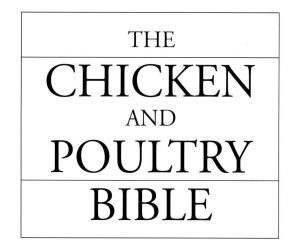

THE

CHICKEN

AND

POULTRY

BIBLE

THE
CHICKEN
AND
POULTRY
BIBLE

The Definitive Sourcebook, with over 800 Illustrations

Christian Teubner
Sybil Gräfin Schönfeldt
Siegfried Scholtyssek

CHARTWELL
BOOKS, INC.

This edition published in 2010 by:
CHARTWELL BOOKS, INC.
A division of BOOK SALES, INC.
276 Fifth Avenue, Suite 206
New York, New York 10001
USA

ISBN-13: 978-0-7858-1908-0
ISBN-10: 0-7858-1908-8

Library of Congress Catalogue Card Number: 97-66092

Original edition:
© 1992 Teubner Edition, Germany

English language translation:
© 1997 Transedition Limited, England
All rights reserved

Printed in Singapore

Contents

As early as 2500 years BC ducks and geese were being kept and fattened as domestic animals, as the reliefs in many Egyptian tombs show.

A short history of poultry

In the beginning

On the fifth day God created "every winged bird," as it is expressed in the King James Version of the Bible (Gen. 1:21), and from that moment on feathered creatures have had their place in biblical history, from the dove that Noah released from the Ark to search for dry land, to the cock that crowed after Peter had betrayed Jesus three times. Whether one believes these stories literally or accepts the views of archeologists and scientists, who have used fossil evidence to trace the origin of modern birds back to the archaeopteryx in the Jurassic Period, the heavens were, either from the fifth day of Creation or a point in time some 180 million years ago, the sole preserve of animals with wings and plumage.

On the sixth day God created "a man and a woman and said unto them, 'Be fruitful and multiply and replenish the earth and subdue it and have dominion … over the fowl of the air…'" Now the geologists and archeologists count out the millions of years for us: the first modern humans appeared late in the Pleistocene Period, and lived for several hundred millennia feeding on grains and fruit, caterpillars and snails, and probably on eggs from nests and hollows. Then people learned to control fire and to use it for cooking, the oldest trail of ashes and charred animal bones yet found dating to about half a million years ago.

From the first farmers to the Middle Ages

Some 8,000 years BC people began to make the transition to a more settled lifestyle, one that would enable them to fulfill those instructions given on the sixth day of Creation: "replenish the earth and subdue it." Gradually, nomadic hunters and gatherers became farmers and stockbreeders, the original food producers; land came under the plow, and animals — first cattle, and, later, poultry — were enclosed within fences and coops. "Have dominion over the fowl of the air." Who was it that first enticed a wild chicken with a handful of grain? Who first dared to tame a goose?

With house and hearth, people had set themselves apart from the hordes that had moved across the face of the earth in search of food. And now the stages of human development are counted in millennia, in centuries, and even in single years; now the fowl of the air are bound up with that development, with the gradual move from small farming communities to towns and cities, from agriculture to industrialization, from farming to factories.

For many people, the idea of raising poultry conjures up an image in which paradise seems to repeat itself: the farmyard, a seemingly timeless place alongside the farmhouse, where the rooster struts and crows, hens and their chicks peck at their food, waddling ducks cackle noisily as they lead the lines of ducklings between the yard and the pond, and geese honk and hiss at unwanted visitors. This, at least, is the modern city-dweller's simple, idyllic view, as depicted in pretty pictures in children's storybooks and idealized scenes in Hollywood movies. The reality, of course, is and always has been more complex.

Anyone keeping animals also has to feed them; protect them from predators and harsh climatic conditions; milk the cattle; collect the eggs from the chickens, ducks, and geese; and, before modern specialization separated these aspects of farming, husband these resources so that there are always some creatures to breed and to provide milk and eggs, and some to slaughter for their meat.

After the so-called agrarian revolution in the Neolithic Period, this interplay of cost and benefit became a problem, and people had to consider the economic viability of what they kept. They became accustomed to settling in communities and sharing the work of producing food, but they were still at the mercy of the climate and of diseases that affected their crops and their livestock, as well as themselves. They sowed and harvested cereals, from which they made breads and porridges. They had to save some of the harvested grain for seed corn for the next spring, and could use only the surplus for feed. If the amount for feed was insufficient, the animals would have to be slaughtered. Cattle needed a great deal of feed over the winter, but poultry were less demanding: a hen could peck around through the leanest days and yet be turned into a fine roast.

A variety of fowl has been eaten around the world for many hundreds, and in some cases thousands, of years. For example, there is evidence that people in Mesoamerica were eating ducks, geese, and other wildfowl between 6000 and 4500 BC, and that people inhabiting the Indus plains may have begun domesticating the Indian jungle fowl, which later became the chicken, sometime around 5000 BC. Tomb paintings from the beginning of the third millennium BC show that the ancient Egyptians ate pigeon stew and quail. Contemporaneous writings reveal that goose and chicken were eaten in ancient Greece as far back as the fifth century BC — indeed, Aristophanes wrote that every Athenian, even the poorest ones, had a hen — while Chinese poetry from the third century BC mentions braised chicken, casseroled duck, and goose cooked in sour sauce as some of the gastronomic delights of the time. By the second century AD, rich Romans were eating chickens and their eggs, and breeding pigeons for the table.

European traditions

Poultry was part of the food supply in Europe throughout the Middle Ages, eaten even by peasants occasionally. It was certainly part of the

The medieval kitchen often served poultry whole. Forks were largely unknown, but, as can be seen here, most people had knives with which to cut up the birds.

tax-in-kind imposed by medieval kings, who traveled their lands frequently and needed fresh food for themselves and their large entourages. For example, in the eighth century the king of Wessex was entitled to be supplied with 10 geese and 20 chickens — as well as varying numbers of sheep, salmon, eel, loaves of bread, and whole cheeses — by any village in his domain in which he stayed. In the middle of the ninth century, Charles the Bald of France ensured that his bishops would not starve on their journeys through the country by ordering that they could requisition 10 chickens and 50 eggs (at a time when hens were not the regular egg producers that they are today) in addition to 50 loaves of bread and 5 suckling pigs from villages on their route. Much later, in the sixteenth century King Henri IV of France entered the history books as a good monarch because, apart from all his other deeds, instead of demanding food from his subjects, he is said to have promised them that there would be no peasant in his kingdom so poor that he could not have a chicken in his pot every Sunday.

In the Middle Ages a young chicken was a portion for one person, as a poussin might be today. It was placed whole onto bread or a tin plate, and there is no Hollywood costume drama set in this period that does not extravagantly depict how men would smash the roast cockerel with their fist and pull apart the meat with their fingers whether they were at a formal banquet, an inn, or a campfire. Illustrations and written records from this period, however, make it clear that some roast meats were brought to the table carved, and that most people carried a dagger-like knife with them and used it to cut their meat and other food into reasonably sized portions that they could then convey to their mouth with their fingers or a spoon.

The festive meals of medieval times were magnificent and impressive because of their sheer extravagance. When English kings celebrated Christmas in the thirteenth and fourteenth centuries, thousands of chickens and — in the case of Henry III — 115 cranes had to lose their lives. For his 6,000 guests, the Archbishop of York ordered the slaughter of 2,000 geese, 1,000 capons, 104 peacocks, and 13,500 birds, all of which were consumed in a few days along with the usual meat, pies, fish, and game. Beggars at the gate of a lord's manor were entitled to leftovers from the table even before the household servants, and the luckiest among them may be presumed to have partaken of such delicacies, if only rarely.

Cooking techniques

As for the taste of these birds, which also included crows, nightingales, storks, and eagles, and how tough or tender they were, we can only guess. However, the slaughter of a "chicken of uncertain age," as it says in old cookbooks, or an elderly hen that was no longer laying did not necessarily mean a dry, leathery roast. While roasting young birds on a spit is a familiar image of the Middle Ages, it was not the only way in which poultry was prepared. Frugality led to the development of cooking methods that made even the toughest birds enjoyable. Slow cooking an old hen stuffed with onions and herbs in a cauldron of water for several hours on the edge of the range or fire produced a tasty broth with a powerful aroma and meat tender enough to be consumed even by someone who had lost their teeth. For a special occasion, the cooked meat could be worked patiently for several hours in a mortar with nuts, oil, and pepper or with garlic, herbs and bacon to produce the basic filling for pies.

For thousands of years the highly developed culinary art of China has held the meat of ducks and chickens in particularly high esteem. Chinese peasants today take their birds to market in almost the same way as their ancestors did more than 100 years ago.

The popularity and variety of poultry in Europe throughout the Middle Ages are reflected in this painting, completed in 1570, by the Dutchman Joachim Buckelaar (Museum voor Schone Kunsten, Ghent).

Excess and imagination

The wasteful abundance of the late fifteenth and sixteenth centuries entered the cultural history books because of the imagination of the cooks. Food was now intended not only to satisfy the appetite, but also to symbolize the splendor of life, enhance the prestige of the host, and arouse envy. In a time before newspapers, when information and gossip were passed from person to person, meals were designed to so astonish and impress all the senses that guests and servants, and even beggars, would continue to speak of them for a long time afterward. Our understanding of what such occasions were like comes mainly from the domestic records of noble households and monasteries. Thus, for example, we know that as trumpets were blown and banners were waved, servants carried to the table gilded cases containing roasted birds artificially clad in their own feathers and lying on a bed of flowers — perhaps swans, which smelled of the spices of the orient under their white plumage, or peacocks, with their tails fanned, stuffed with roast

thrushes. There might be, as in the nursery rhyme, enormous pies that, when opened, released live birds flapping gilded wings, or a boned swan containing a boned capon, which, in turn, contained a chicken, itself stuffed with a thrush or a pigeon, concealing a lark containing a tiny charm made from pure gold.

All the dishes for the first course were put on the table at the same time, although a course then was a more or less random assortment rather than the harmonious grouping of foods into distinct sections of a meal that we are used to today. Dishes were replaced or added to by the servants on their next run (the word "course" is derived from the Latin "*curs*," meaning "run") from the often very distant kitchen. The first course might include partridges with figs, and capons with sorrel and almond cakes, and the second might also contain chicken and other poultry. There was no appetizer or dessert, no coordination of dishes, no alternation of ingredients; the meal was a pure display of power and magnificence.

The magnificent cockerel – a symbol of fertility and simultaneously a harvest cock, weather cock, and fighting cock – has always been a popular motif in art.

New influences

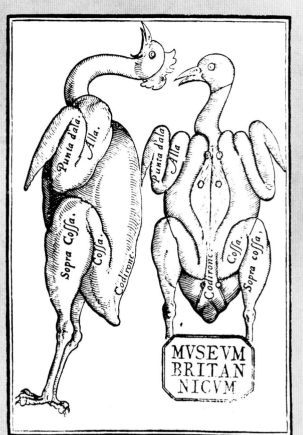

Exotic birds like the "Indian cock" or a magnificent peacock were the culinary showpieces on princely tables in seventeenth-century Europe.

In the sixteenth century cooks in Italy began to adapt to the rising price of imported spices by producing food that was simpler and more natural. The variety of poultry available contributed to the diversity of the menu. Plain and stuffed, spit-roasted and boiled, larks and quails, pigeons and partridges, chickens and geese were now flavored with local herbs and served with simple sauces and vegetables. It is possible that the subsequent changes in French cuisine were influenced by these developments in Italy, particularly as Catherine de' Medici and, later, Marie de' Medici both brought Italian cooks to the royal kitchens of France. Books of recipes were published (although nowhere near as many as in the present day) and new ideas about cooking spread.

Cuisine in different countries was also affected by location and climate, and the availability of ingredients. Explorers and other travelers brought to their own countries plants and animals from the lands they had visited, and international traders ensured that some of these items reached a wider market. Thus, the turkey, a native of Central and North America, was first brought to Spain from Mexico in the early sixteenth century, and

Fresh food

Meat was difficult to keep without refrigeration. There was no adequate protection against mildew or flies, and the only methods of preservation were salting, which was expensive, and drying, which was not always possible. Poultry, therefore, and particularly chicken, had a great advantage: it represented a living store. The birds were always at hand, did not need to be hung for long, if at all, after being killed, and were small enough to be cooked whole for immediate consumption. Leftovers could be preserved by pouring liquid fat or oil over them or by placing them in honey or vinegar. Chicken was prepared in this way and stored in barrels covered with sailcloth as provisions for seafarers.

In general, there was still no call for fresh and unspoiled food. It may be that the pungency of the spices and the acidity of vinegar and wine used to mask the mustiness of the flour, the rancidness of the fat, and the gamey taste of the meat had influenced people's taste so much that they did not value the natural flavor of the food, but admired the art of the cooks, who gave everything a similar taste.

In medieval Europe chickens and ducks were cooked on a rotating spit over glowing charcoal — a method that is still unsurpassable today.

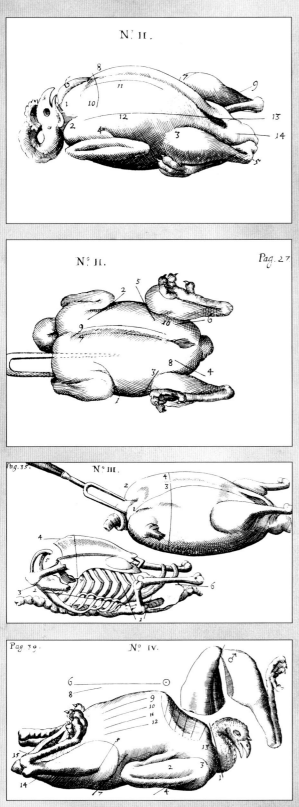

The illustrations above appeared in the *New Booklet on Carving*, which was published in Nürnberg in 1677. It describes "How, in the present court manner, all types of foods and fruits can be artistically cut, presented, served ...". The four drawings show the noble art of "carving roast chicken" (top), "carving roast chicken, capon, or goose in a new and refined way" (second), "a different and comfortable way with goose" (third) and "carving a turkey" (above).

probably was introduced to other European countries from there by traveling merchants. It was certainly established in England by the middle of the century, and so was familiar to the Pilgrims who founded Plymouth Colony in 1620.

From our earliest school days we hear the story of how more than half the colonists died in that first harsh winter, for which they were so ill-prepared, and how the remainder would have starved without the support of the local Native Americans, who taught them to cultivate — and cook — the indigenous plants and animals. So when a reasonable harvest was forecast the following summer, Governor William Bradford declared a harvest festival to give thanks to God, and invited the Native Americans to join them. Tradition has it that the turkey became the centerpiece of our annual Thanksgiving celebrations from that day forth, and eventually displaced the goose as the Christmas roast.

The celebration goose

For centuries in Europe November marked the end of the peasant year. The animals were driven in from the pasture, and those that did not spend the winter in the protection of the coop or stall were slaughtered, processed, and stored to provide food throughout the cold, dark months to come. A good year was regarded as an omen of prosperity for the next year, and people celebrated with a feast. Since very early times people had regarded the fat goose as the blessing of the Earth Goddess, a symbol of fertility, and so it became the feature of these harvest festivals of thanksgiving.

Later, the goose became associated with both St. Michael in England, and St. Martin elsewhere in Europe. The feast of St. Michael and All Angels is celebrated on September 29, and the custom of eating goose on this day probably began because geese were generally plentiful and in good condition at this time of year. Many stories were invented to explain the connection between the goose and St. Martin. According to one, Martin, when he was Bishop of Tours in the fourth century, was so disturbed during a sermon by the cackling of a goose that he ordered it to be killed and cooked for his dinner, and thereafter a goose was sacrificed in his honor on his saint's day, November 11. This day was marked in the old Norwegian runic calendars and, until some time in the last century, in the Tyrolean peasant calendar simply by a painted goose.

The tradition of the Christmas goose began in

The more lavish the pie, the higher the standing of the cook. The greatest art, however, lay in bringing the birds to the table fully cooked, yet giving them as natural an appearance as possible.

Mugwort was, and in some places still is, used in stuffings for geese and ducks because it is good for the stomach, helps to digest fat, and prevents cramps.

England, and although we do not know when or why, some sources claim that this custom was established by Queen Elizabeth I; perhaps the queen simply liked this rich dark meat and her subjects followed suit.

The modern era

Before the Industrial Revolution 90 percent of the population of Europe was engaged in agriculture, and even people living in towns kept cows, pigs, and hens until the sixteenth century. Children knew the hens that laid the breakfast eggs, and in the early summer they would hold the chicks and goslings in their laps. Later, when the fluffy gray goslings turned into smooth, white geese, and when they spat and gaggled and unfolded their enormous strong wings as if to fly, or when downy yellow chicks grew into stout cockerels with strong beaks, there could scarcely have been a child who was not frightened of them, and thus cried no sentimental tears when it came time to eat them.

In most communities looking after the poultry was one of the duties of the housewife. In many cases this meant she not only collected the eggs, but also took them to market, thereby earning her a small amount of money and a measure of independence. She might be able to exchange a chicken for a piece of material too, efficiently managing the resources of her household economy; for centuries this was, and for many people continues to be, based on the principle of not wasting anything, of finding a sensible use for everything.

Wherever poultry was bred, people appreciated it for more than its meat. There were the eggs, of course, but the feathers, too, had their valued uses: quills for writing, and down for bedding and clothing. Feather-splicing was winter work. All the feathers that had been accumulated in the course of the year from plucking the geese, chickens, and ducks were brought together, and the women of the household would sit down with the children and, perhaps, with the neighbors to tear the feathers from the quills. The tough feathers were stuffed into featherbeds, and ruffled down was put into pillows and used to make warm quilted clothes — just what was needed in the cold indoors and on the long winter journeys on foot.

In the eighteenth and nineteenth centuries some poultry was accorded yet another role. The defensive walls of towns and fortresses had become superfluous; villas and houses had become possible, and were surrounded by open parks. These now became the backdrop for peacock and golden pheasant, guinea fowl and quail. Ponds became the place for swans and ducks: animals for decoration but also a food supply, just as previously the pigeon lofts in the castles had delighted the eye but been designed as emergency stores for long sieges.

Looking after poultry was still women's work. In Germany toward the end of the nineteenth century, townswomen were given advice on how to breed, feed, and care for domestic poultry. For raising guinea fowl, they were told they should use the park lawns, but keep peacocks on the paths. The women had to bear in mind that since the peahens did not brood normally, it was up to them to place these neglected eggs under a domestic hen at the right time. Good housewives not only had to prepare ant pupa, grubs, and beetles as peacock food, and carefully mix onions into the usual poultry feed of corn, curds, and leek, they also had to cure pigeons and chickens, turkeys and ducks of digestive complaints, and treat them for mites and fleas by administering doses of particular herbs, tincture of malic acid and iron, or peppercorns and wine, or by applying ointments or embrocations of poppy-seed oil or soft soap. Diligent housewives had no less work with the pigeons, but it was considered more enjoyable, as "for the sentient person there is something uncommonly charming about caring for these beautiful, gentle, and clean birds..."

The present day

Parks and municipal gardens throughout the world still play host to a variety of fowl, but towns and cities soon became too densely populated for people to continue rearing their own poultry. As more people moved to the cities, there were fewer people to work on the land, and yet there was an increased

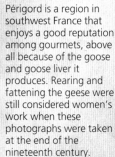

Périgord is a region in southwest France that enjoys a good reputation among gourmets, above all because of the goose and goose liver it produces. Rearing and fattening the geese were still considered women's work when these photographs were taken at the end of the nineteenth century.

demand for food from the growing population. New farming methods and machines, distribution and storage facilities, and other technological advances ensured that, in the industrialized countries at least, there was, and continues to be sufficient food to supply the population. In the process many animals, and particularly poultry, have been deprived of their natural environment and turned into an industrial product: the barnyard hen has become the factory chicken, quality has been sacrificed for quantity, flavor and texture for availability. However, people who are concerned about the food they eat, who know that the quality of the dish is dependent on the quality of the ingredients, and who are concerned about the conditions in which animals are kept, have stimulated a return to natural farming and proved there is a large and growing market for flavorful poultry.

All about poultry

Poultry has been an important part of the diet of all peoples since ancient times. Today, because of its high-protein and, in many cases, low-fat content, and its great culinary versatility, it is the most popular of meats. In terms of quantity, the chicken family is the undisputed leader, coming way ahead of other types of poultry. Chickens of all sizes and ages, from the tiny poussin up to the large roaster, are available all year around. The larger birds are sold whole and in portions, fresh and frozen, and are the basis of many chilled and frozen prepared meals.

Like chickens, turkeys are reared both traditionally and intensively. Their production has increased markedly in recent times because their body size and carcass weight are more favorable than those of chickens, they are very low in fat, and they are particularly good for processing.

Guinea fowl, squab, and quail are the elite poultry (a fact that is usually reflected in the price), the smaller birds, for people with culinary imagination and adventurous palates. Duck and goose are prized for their strong, distinctive taste, which develops particularly well during cooking as a result of their relatively high fat content.

High-quality poultry requires that other ingredients should also be of the highest standard,
for example the red wine in this marinade.

increases significantly with age, while the proportion of meat on the wings and back decreases.

The characteristics of body growth and body structure are, to a large extent, inherited, factors that are important in breeding fattening birds. The majority of fattened chickens, turkeys and ducks are now bred using a type of hybrid breeding called a "three-way cross." In this process birds from two medium-weight breeds or lines that both have vigorous growth and good laying qualities (1 and 2 in the diagram below) are crossed and produce chicks with improved vitality and, in the case of the females, enhanced laying capabilities. The resulting strong and prolific hens are then paired with very heavy and well-proportioned cocks (3 in the diagram below), chosen particularly for their large breasts and legs, to produce the desired fattening chicks. When selecting birds for breeding, the breeders take into consideration the principles of genetic interaction and sex-linked effects as well as the characteristics, such as weight development, laying yield (in the case of female animals) and vitality, that they wish to enhance and maintain in each generation.

Farmyard hens are kept primarily for laying eggs. When these hens are no longer productive, the quality of their meat is good enough only for soup, for which its strong flavor makes it particularly suitable.

Chickens like these are bred for their meat, and will be sold as young fattened birds.

Breeding
The quest for higher yield and better taste

All types of poultry offered for human consumption are bred particularly for their meat yield and are sold as young fattened birds. Sexually mature parent or breeding birds, like the majority of boiling fowl, can be used only in soups or conserves, or possibly for stewing. During rearing, special attention is paid to the breast and leg, which are the areas richest in meat. The breast is formed predominantly from the large and small breast muscle, and the leg comprises many cords of muscle. Quail has the largest proportion of breast meat in relation to its whole body, followed by turkey, guinea fowl, chicken, goose, and duck. In the case of leg meat, chicken is in first place, followed by guinea fowl, turkey, goose, duck, and quail. The age of the animal is important. In chickens and turkeys the proportion of breast meat

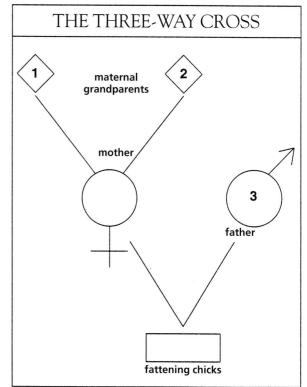

THE THREE-WAY CROSS

1
2
maternal grandparents
mother
3
father
fattening chicks

Hybrid breeding. The proportions of usable meat, the relative sizes of individual parts, and other characteristics are weighted differently for the three lines.

Table 1: Weights of young fattened birds			
Type of poultry	Fattening time (weeks)	Live weight (lb) m f	Dressed carcass (%)
Chicken	6	4 3½	70
	8	6 5	72
Turkey	12	16 13	77
	18	30 22	80
	24	44	82
Pekin duck	8	7	70
Muscovy duck	8	7 4½	72
	10	9 6	74
Goose	12	12 10	73
	16	14 12	74
	20	16½ 14	75
Guinea fowl	8	3	–
	12	4	–
Squab	4	1	–
Quail	6–8	½	–

The weight of fattened poultry varies widely, according to breeding, age, and sex. All the data shown in Table 1 are rough average values. In the case of chicken, a standard type of hybrid has been developed that at 38–40 days weighs approximately 4 pounds and thus supplies the bulk of the demand for chicken for the domestic consumer.

Prolonged fattening makes it possible to guarantee better meat quality. In the case of turkey, this means heavy, wide-breasted birds. Baby turkeys are of only limited significance, because they have to compete with the large chickens and thus become uneconomic. Turkeys are fattened for different lengths of time according to sex; the female turkey achieves the optimum weight between 12 and 18 weeks, after which added weight is a result of increased fat content, which is not desirable.

Table 1 includes two types of duck: Pekin (or Peking), a popular breed of the mallard family (from which the majority of domestic ducks are descended); and muscovy, the only other family of duck to be domesticated. Pekin ducks are fattened for up to eight weeks and reach an average weight of 6½ pounds. Muscovy ducks have better body proportioning (more breast), less fat, and a more distinctive, more gamey taste. In these ducks sexual dimorphism increases markedly with age, so the males and females are fattened separately from an early stage.

There is a great variation in weight in the geese that reach the market, which is not apparent from the table, according to the different breeds and the type of rearing — rapid fattening, intensive, or pasture fattening. Pasture-fattened geese can be reared for significantly longer (until they are six months old) than those that are reared in the other ways without adding much more weight.

Table 1 provides only an approximate guide to the average weight of guinea fowl, squab, and quail, which can be very different according to breed.

How many servings?

The number of servings any type of poultry will provide depends, of course, on, first, whether it is intended as an appetizer, as a filling main dish, or as a meat entrée in a menu of several courses; and, second, on the other ingredients in the recipe. The number of servings shown in Table 2 is intended as a rough guide when the meat is being used in a meat course with other ingredients.

Table 2: Number of servings				
Type of poultry	Weight (lb)	Breast (%)	Leg (%)	Number of portions
Light chicken	2½	32	36	2–3
Heavy chicken	5	34	36	3–4
Light turkey	5½	41	30	5–7
Heavy turkey	30	48	31	–
Pekin duck	4	24	24	3–5
Muscovy duck	4½	30	23	3–6
Goose	8	30	23	6–8
Guinea fowl	3	32	29	3–4
Squab	¾	40	15	1
Quail	¼	40	27	½

In many markets in Asia and Latin America, and in some southern European countries, the customers can select their poultry from among the living animals on sale. The choice is wide, but the animals are not always of very good quality.

The presentation of any product must attract customers, and it is with this in mind that the poultry is presented in the shops and markets. In Hong Kong (below) this includes the prepared giblets, heads, and feet. In Mexico (right) chickens are judged more on their yellow color.

La Boqueria in Barcelona, is one of many modern covered markets in Europe where poultry is displayed in this traditional manner.

Processing

How the poultry comes to market

Once upon a time shoppers went to their local butcher or poulterer, chose a bird and had it slaughtered and prepared while they waited. This still happens in many parts of the world, but in most large, modern industrialized countries, factory-farmed poultry is processed into oven-ready birds or portions at the factory where it was reared.

In a modern poultry processing plant most of the handling is carried out by machines, which reduces the risk of dangerous infection. In particular, the opening, gutting and cleaning of the abdominal cavity are carried out far more hygienically than would be possible manually. After these basic procedures, the carcasses are packed, with or without giblets, labeled and then sent, fresh or frozen, to stores and supermarkets.

While sales of whole poultry are constantly rising, there is also an increased demand for portions — packages of chicken halves, quarters, wings, drumsticks, and boned breasts. Butchers at the supermarket can cut whole chickens into portions manually to meet an individual customer's needs. For example, they can quickly cut the bird in half or in quarters, or separate the legs at the hip and knee joints to produce drumsticks and thigh portions; they can detach the wings at the shoulder joint, and then separate the two halves of the breast from the thorax with a single cut along the breast bone. This is all right if a customer wants all the portions of the bird, or if the customer who wants only the breast quarters is matched by one who wants only the leg quarters, but it is not efficient for the supermarket if too many customers want the service and if the majority of them want the same portions. The only practical way supermarkets can meet the daily large-scale demand for selected portions is to buy them in this form from commercial producers. The same producers who prepare whole birds for the market use cutting machines, which have either a straight or circular saw, set to a certain caliber, or body structure, to perform all the cutting operations much more quickly. The supermarkets can then order the right quantity of each portion to meet the changing demand.

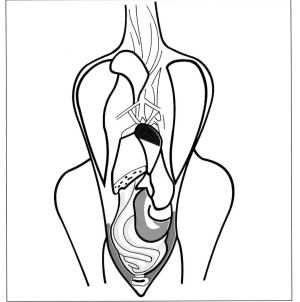

Low in fat, high in protein
Poultry in the modern diet

Health experts advise us that a healthy diet should be low in fat and cholesterol and provide certain amounts of protein, vitamins, and minerals every day. For most people, the biggest proportion of fat in the diet comes from meat. Poultry has gained in popularity in recent years because, as well as being versatile and tasty, it is low in fat and provides significant amounts of the required protein, vitamins, and minerals. For example, the ratio of fat in the breast meat of chicken compared with equivalent muscle meat in beef and pork is 1:4:6 — which means it is also lower in calories — and the ratio of protein is 1:0.9:0.7. It also has a comparatively high vitamin C and magnesium content.

Table 3 shows how the different types of poultry compare with each other in nutritional terms. The digestibility of poultry depends on its fat content. Thus the so-called "lean poultry" (chicken, turkey, quail, and squab) is easily digestible and lower in calories, whereas the "fat poultry" (duck and goose) is harder to digest as well as higher in calories. However, although duck and goose have a higher fat content than chicken, a large proportion of it is in the form of the dietetically desirable unsaturated fatty acids, which is also the case with turkey.

The fat distribution in the body of a chicken. In an oven-ready chicken, the giblets along with the fat from the heart, stomach, and intestines, highlighted in color in the diagram, have been removed. Only the abdominal fat, which can easily be removed before preparation, and the intramuscular fat remain in the body.

Table 3: Nutritional value

An edible portion of 3½ ounces contains:

Type of poultry	Protein (g)	Fat (g)	Energy (Kcal/kJ)	Ca (mg)	P (mg)	K (mg)	Na (mg)	Fe (mg)	A (µg)	B₁ (µg)	B₂ (µg)	Niacin (mg)
Young fattened chicken	20.6	5.6	144/602	12	200	359	82	1.8	39	83	160	6
Breast	22.8	0.9	109/457	14	212	264	66	1.1	60	70	90	10
Leg	20.6	2.4	113/473	15	188	250	95	1.8	150	100	240	5
Liver	22.1	4.7	142/594	18	240	218	68	7.4	12,800	320	2,490	11
Boiling fowl	18.5	20.3	274/1,147	11	178	400	50	1.4	32	60	170	9
Large turkey	20.2	15.0	231/968	25	226	300	63	1.4	13	100	180	8
Young turkey	22.4	6.8	163/682	26	238	315	66	1.5	–	80	140	8
Breast	24.1	1.0	115/483	–	–	333	46	1.0	+	47	81	11
Leg	20.5	3.6	124/521	–	–	289	86	2.0	+	90	180	5
Duck	18.1	17.2	243/1,017	11	187	292	80	2.1	•	300	200	•
Goose	15.7	31.0	364/1,521	12	184	420	86	1.9	65	120	260	•
Quail	22.4	2.3	120/504	14	179	280	46	–	•	130	170	•
Squab	20.9	9.5	182/762	45	217	330	90	–	•	100	280	•

Ca = Calcium, P = Phosphorous, K = Potassium, Na = Sodium, Fe = Iron
• not stated   – not present   + traces

Chilling and freezing

An important quality criterion for all food is its freshness or storage life. The way in which poultry is stunned and killed, and the technological means used, amongst other things, for chilling and freezing determine how rapidly rigor mortis sets in. These "braking functions" affect the biochemical transformations in the muscle and thus also the state of the muscle fibers, that is, the tenderness of the meat. Painstaking hygiene in the slaughtering process precludes any contact with bacteria, and rapid cooling or freezing improves storage life.

After slaughter and gutting, birds that are to be sold fresh are cleaned and then chilled by air-spray chilling — the preferred method — air chilling, or water-immersion chilling. The birds are then kept at a storage temperature of 32–35°F until they are bought by the consumer. This temperature must be maintained without variation until the meat is prepared for consumption. In these conditions the carcasses stay fresh for seven days.

Commercial deep-freezing guarantees perfect, high-quality meat that tastes as good as the fresh product. During the slaughtering process, poultry that is to be frozen is blanched and roughly plucked. After gutting and cleaning, the poultry is immediately chilled and then rapidly deep frozen to a core temperature of 0°F — the freezing point of food is lower than that of pure water. Poultry, which contains a gelatinous substance in its cells, must be frozen very quickly so that only uniform, minute ice crystals form throughout the body. Then when the bird is thawed, the cells can reabsorb the liquid produced by the melting crystals. Once frozen, the poultry must be stored at a constant temperature no higher than 0°F, and preferably lower, from –10 to –30°F. Fluctuations in storage temperatures can encourage larger ice crystals to develop, which puncture the cells, making it impossible for them to reabsorb the liquid when the poultry is thawing. As a result, the meat will be drier, tougher and have less flavor.

Buying a bird fresh and then freezing it at home is not as good as using it fresh or buying a deep-frozen bird. Although some home freezers have a quick-freeze facility, most freezers do not freeze food as quickly, or necessarily to the same temperature, as commercial ones. This relatively slow freezing results in the formation of the undesirable large ice crystals Although it is, therefore, better to buy poultry that is already deep-frozen, it may nonetheless, sometimes be necessary to freeze fresh poultry. In this case, be sure to wrap it carefully. The smallest

To prepare poultry for cooking:

Allow the washed poultry to drain thoroughly, turning it so that the water also drains from the abdominal cavity.

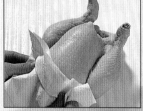

Carefully pat dry, inside and out, with a linen cloth or paper towels.

Always wash poultry very carefully inside and out.

Table 4: Thawing times for deep-frozen poultry			
Type of poultry	Refrigerator (39°F)	Room (68°F) hours	Microwave minutes
Quail	2–3	1–2	5–6
Squab	5–8	2–3	20–30
Broiler	12–18	5–7	30–40
Roaster	22–25	12–15	40–60
Guinea fowl	22–25	12–15	40–60
Pekin duck	22–35	12–15	40–60
Muscovy duck	28–35	15–18	100–170
Goose	35–38	16–20	160–240
Baby turkey	35–38	16–20	180–260

To thaw poultry:

Cut open the packaging, remove it completely and discard it.

Place the poultry in a large container with a rack or sieve insert, cover and thaw slowly in the refrigerator.

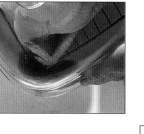

Pour away the thawing water. Do not allow it to come into contact with other foods, as there is a risk of salmonella.

hole in the wrapping will always result in freezerburn. You can freeze individual portions, such as the legs or breast, more successfully: because of their smaller size the cold can penetrate more quickly. Again, it is important to make sure that the wrapping is not damaged in any way, particularly by protruding bones.

The maximum storage times for deep-frozen poultry stored at 0°F are: chicken, 1 year; turkey, 1½ years; goose and duck, 8 months. The shorter storage time for goose and duck reflects the fact that waterfowl have a higher fat content, and while freezing does, to a large extent, impede the process of fat turning rancid, it is unable to prevent this from happening altogether.

Thawing

All frozen meat products should be thawed slowly and completely, ideally in a refrigerator. Rapid freezing and slow thawing put the least stress on the cell walls, so that only small quantities of tissue fluid are released and the meat does not taste too dry. The thawing time depends on the carcass weight. Table

A meat thermometer is useful for precisely measuring the temperature inside the meat. A core temperature of at least 176°F, and preferably 194°F, is required. Do not measure next to the bone, as the temperature there is considerably higher than in the meat.

4 shows the thawing time of deep-frozen birds, starting with the smallest, the quail. Birds can be thawed rapidly in a microwave; the times given for this in the table include both operating and waiting time, and are for medium-powered machines. Manufacturers of some fan-assisted ovens also give instructions on thawing meat. Whichever method is used, it is important that the poultry is completely thawed before cooking or it will not cook all the way through. All poultry should also be washed thoroughly before cooking.

Salmonella

Salmonella is one of the bacteria that cause food poisoning. It occurs in many food animals, but people associate it most frequently with poultry. Indeed, the skin of poultry, which is moist and rich in protein, is an ideal germinating ground for salmonella. Maintaining the highest standard of hygiene in the working environment — at the commercial producers, at the supermarket, and at home — is the first line of protection against the spread of any bacteria. The surest method of killing salmonella is to cook poultry thoroughly. It is important not to rely only on the cooking times stated in the recipes, but to test the meat to see if it is cooked. Poultry is cooked when the meat comes away from the bone and the juices run clear when the thickest part of the meat is pierced. Another reliable way to check is to measure the temperature at the core (see illustration, left).

Freezerburn is a quality defect in deep-frozen products. If the packaging is damaged, the meat under the hole dries as a result of the freeze-drying effect. White spots are a typical sign.

Chicken

Galliformes

The chicken (*Gallus gallus*) is one of the oldest living species of animal. It is assumed that the domestic chicken (*Gallus domesticus*) and all subsequent breeds are descended from the Bankiva chicken (*Gallus bankiva*), also known as the red-crested chicken or jungle chicken. This native of Malaysia, India, and China, is still found there in the wild. It spread from these areas to the whole of Asia, Africa, and Europe, ultimately becoming one of the most useful and popular domestic animals throughout the world. It lays eggs, which are eaten in their own right and are used in cooking other foods, and it provides tender, tasty, and easily digestible meat. Because of this range of excellent culinary characteristics, the chicken has maintained its place in all the cuisines of the world and is constantly giving rise to new recipes.

When consumers speak of "chicken," they generally mean young fattened, sexually immature chickens of either gender. At one time commercial chickens were bred for both laying (to supply eggs) and fattening (to supply meat), but today these objectives are pursued separately, and the chickens that we eat are different breeds from those whose eggs we consume. This book is concerned only with the birds we eat, and more familiar to us than the names of the breeds are the descriptions of the bird according to age, weight and cooking method. The youngest are six weeks old, and are called poussins. Chickens between two and four months old and weighing about 2½ pounds were once referred to as spring chickens but now are more commonly known as broilers; slightly larger ones (up to 3½ pounds) of the same age are called fryers. Roasters are between four and seven months old and weigh between 3½ and 5 pounds.

Farming methods

The high demand for poultry meat and the need for a rapid and high-quality supply has led to the development of the large-scale business referred to as intensive or factory farming. Breeding and processing chickens from egg to finished product tend to be separate, specialized operations. Thus breeders select the particular breeds and lines that will provide the best end product, and send the resultant hatching eggs to the producers. In factory farming, eggs are hatched in incubators, which are regulated to maintain the optimum temperature (100°F), humidity, air flow, and balance of oxygen and carbon dioxide for the embryo to grow, and which turn the eggs mechanically to prevent malformation or death of the embryos. The chicks are well-developed by the time they hatch in twenty-one days.

In intensive farming of broilers, the chickens are

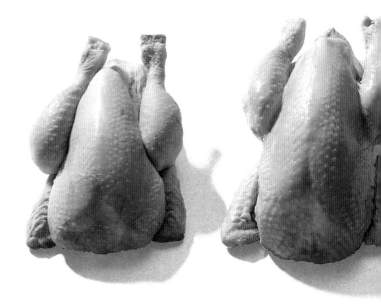

Broiler   **Fryer**

kept in cages — three to ten chickens to a cage, and three tiers of cages — while they are fattened. Feeding, watering, and cleaning are highly mechanized operations, making it possible for one person to care for as many as 20,000 birds at a time. Broilers gain more than forty-three times their initial weight and reach market size in eight weeks.

As a result of pressure from environmentalists and consumers in some markets, an increasing number of chickens are being reared in more open surroundings to imitate the advantages of natural rearing. In some cases this means that the chickens are raised indoors but not in cages; in others, it means that they have access to the outdoors for the second half of their life. These so-called free range birds have a slower growth rate than those intensively farmed, and so are reared for longer before coming to market.

Chicken feed

Although in the traditional image of the barnyard, chickens are tossed a few handfuls of grain, the diet of the modern chicken is a carefully controlled combination of vitamins (A, C, D, E, K, and all twelve B vitamins), minerals (calcium, chlorine, cobalt, iron, magnesium, manganese, potassium, sodium, sulfur, and zinc), protein, and water. The chicken also requires sources of energy, which come from grains and waste-fats from meat and vegetable oil processing. Antibiotics are included in the feed in the early stages of rearing to prevent disease and to enhance appetite. The composition of the feed affects particularly the bird's rate of growth and the degree of fat in its meat.

Factors affecting the quality of meat

The quality of a chicken can be defined in various ways. For the consumer, in addition to value for money, nutritional value, taste, texture, appearance, and aroma are also decisive. These criteria can be affected by a large number of factors during production and processing. Breeding determines the body structure, including the tissue structure and the body proportions. Older and heavier animals have a higher carcass dressing percentage, a better ratio of meat to bone, a higher proportion of edible parts. Moreover, the ratio of essential to non-essential amino acids and that of unsaturated to saturated fatty acids is more favorable. The taste also improves, although only up to about the twelfth week of life.

The amount of fat in poultry meat is affected not only by the feed the birds consume, but also by their age and sex, and the way they are reared. Little movement leads to excessive fat, while a lot of movement promotes the development of the musculature used for walking and a clear differentiation in the color and texture of the breast and leg muscles.

Roaster   **Boiling fowl**   **Capon**

1 Free the leg first by carefully cutting the skin between the body and the leg with a large sharp knife.

2 Cut through the skin as far as the joint, bending the leg outwards with the hand.

3 Twist the leg until the ball of the joint springs out. Cut through the joint, pressing lightly.

4 Cut through the leg at the knee joint to separate the thigh from the drumstick.

5 Separate the wing at the shoulder joint, cutting off a small part of the breast with it.

6 Press quite firmly to split the collarbone and divide the back parallel to the backbone.

7 Cut across the back at the middle point, breaking the backbone with short movements of the knife.

8 To separate the breasts, carefully cut left and right along the length of the breastbone.

To cut poultry into individual portions simply:

Cutting up poultry
Two methods

The main advantages of cutting up poultry yourself are that it is more economical than buying portions — whole birds cost less than the individual parts — and you can cut the portions the way you want them: drumsticks with or without the thigh, breasts with or without the wing, or various combinations. The technique is easy to learn. The most important point to remember is to feel the joints when you have to sever sinews and cartilage. A serrated knife or poultry shears are ideal for cutting through bone.

The two methods shown here are illustrated with a chicken but are the same for all types of poultry. The method shown on the left is simple and popular with home cooks. The method on the opposite page is used by professional cooks for poultry weighing more than 1¾ pounds, in order to obtain portions of equal size. Here the tender "chicken oysters," whose quality matches that of the breasts, are cut from the back. The legs are left in one piece and, for the sake of appearance, the wing tips are removed.

To cut poultry into individual portions professionally:

1 Make a cut approximately ⅜-inch deep across the back under the shoulder blades.

2 Cut along the backbone at a right angle to this and remove the "chicken oysters."

3 Cut through the skin between the body and the leg. Splay out the leg and cut through the joint.

4 Chop off the outermost section of each wing, cutting through the joint with a small chopper or large knife.

5 Remove the wings with some breast meat — along the breastbone and wishbone as far as the joint.

6 To remove the breasts, first hold the chicken firmly by the wishbone and cut along the breastbone.

7 Turn the carcass 180°, then loosen the breast from the front along the wishbone as far as the joint.

8 Take off the breast, making a cut from the joint to the end of the breastbone.

The number of individual pieces depends on the size of the poultry. You can use the remainder of the carcass to make stock, soups, and sauces.

SPLIT AND PRESS FLAT
Prepared in this way, even larger birds can be broiled, grilled, and roasted evenly, because the heat can penetrate better than in a closed carcass.

1 Lay the chicken on the breast and cut along the back with poultry shears about ⅜-inch from the backbone.

2 Cut along the other side of the backbone in the same way. Remove the backbone with the rump and neck.

A good example:
This chicken has an almond crust and was cooked on a rack in the oven. For a 3-pound chicken, this will take a maximum of 40 minutes at 425°F.

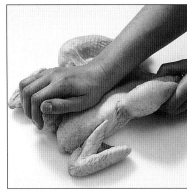

3 Lay the chicken on the board breast uppermost and press down on the breastbone until it stays flat.

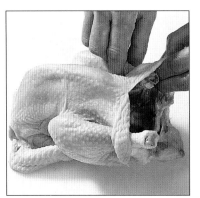

4 Make a hole in the skin either side of the stomach so that you can push the drumsticks through.

Some technique is necessary

Serving poultry that looks right and is evenly cooked through is very easy once some important operations have been mastered. Here are the basic techniques for flattening, trussing, and preparing breasts.

PREPARING FOR BOILING
Chicken can also be dressed in this way for roasting, broiling, or grilling, but with this method the legs do not stay as close as when they are tied.

1 Remove surplus fat and the glands on the skin of the neck, and secure the skin on the back.

2 Use a pointed knife to make a ¾-inch hole in the skin of the stomach to the left and right of the opening.

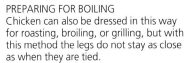

3 Push the ends of the legs through the slits so that they do not splay out during cooking

TRUSSING
This simple technique can be used for all cooking methods except barbecuing. Stuffed chicken, too, whether sewn up or skewered, will keep its shape this way.

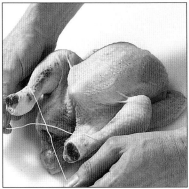

1 Tuck in the wings. Take the string under and around the end of the legs and cross over at the joints.

2 Take the string down the side of the chicken along the legs to the wings and pull tight.

3 Pull the string around to the side of the chicken, making sure that it does not slip, then tie securely.

TAKING OFF THE BREASTS INDIVIDUALLY
This technique is used mainly for chicken and guinea fowl. It can also be used for delicate entrées of squab and quail, but that requires great precision. You can use various forcemeats for stuffing, as well as ham or, as shown here, cheese.

1 Splay out the thigh, cut through at the joint, and remove the leg. Repeat on the other side.

2 Cut into the wings at the elbow joint and sever, taking care not to damage the bones.

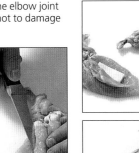

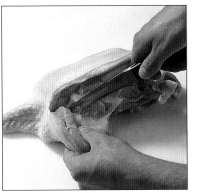

3 Loosen the breast meat from the carcass on either side along the breastbone. Sever the wing at the joint.

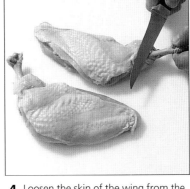

4 Loosen the skin of the wing from the bone and scrape it toward the breast with the back of the knife.

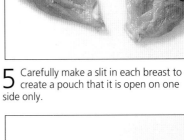

5 Carefully make a slit in each breast to create a pouch that it is open on one side only.

Season the breast with salt and pepper, and fill it, for example, with a piece of cheese. Sear in a frying pan and continue to cook in a preheated oven at 350°F for 12–15 minutes. Allow to rest briefly, then slice.

BONING THE BREASTS IN ONE PIECE
The whole boneless breast can be stuffed, folded together, tied, and then roasted, steamed or coated in breadcrumbs and fried. First remove the legs and two outermost sections of each wing as shown above.

1 Remove all the skin completely from the breast and carefully cut through the joint in the wings.

2 Cut along the wishbone on both sides, free the meat with the fingers and remove it.

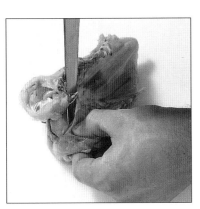

3 Using the tip of the knife, cut along the collarbones and remove them.

4 Holding the breasts firmly, pull out the breastbone, removing the ribs with it.

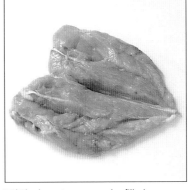

5 The breasts can now be filled as desired and folded together or rolled.

Quail still live in the wild as well as being bred on farms.

Quail for sale in a rural French market.

Quail
Perdicinae

The European quail (*Coturnix coturnix*) is 7 inches long and is found in the temperate zones of the whole of Europe, particularly in Italy, Spain, Greece, and southern Russia, and as far east as Asia. It is the only migratory gallinaceous bird, and in the fall it flies to North Africa. The Japanese quail (*Coturnix japonica*) is almost 6 inches long, and is native to the Japanese islands and to eastern Asia; it winters in southern China. These birds are, in fact, the smallest partridges. There are several species of native American quail, including the bobwhite (*Colinus virginianus*) in the eastern United States, and the California quail (*Lophortyx californicus*) in the west, which are larger than the European species.

Quail are timid animals that are nimble on the ground and in flight. They can climb almost vertically, like helicopters. They have a short neck and a short tail. The plumage on the back of the European quail is yellowish-gray with black spots and yellow feather shafts. A pale-yellow stripe can be clearly seen on the top of the head and above the eyes. The legs are brown and yellowish-white below, and the cocks have no spur. The smaller males have dark back feathers and a light throat (bib). The plumage on the American bobwhite is brown and white on a gray body.

As a commercially useful animal, the Japanese quail occupies a prime position. It became a domestic animal in Japan and China around 1300, when it was kept as a songbird. Only in the twentieth century did its high laying capacity lead people to breed quail for its eggs (250 to 300 eggs per year with an average weight of ½ ounce). Since the middle of the 1950s the Japanese quail has also established itself in Europe, especially in Italy and France, and has been gaining ground as a breeding animal in America too.

On the breeding farms quail are usually kept in cages, for hygienic reasons. They are sexually mature at six weeks. In quails bred for meat, the females are heavier than the males from around the third week, whereas in all the other species of commercial poultry the males are heavier. Female quails are, therefore, slaughtered at five weeks, when they have reached the market weight of 6 ounces, and males at six weeks. The meat yield is then at its best; later the proportion of fat increases sharply. Forty percent of the meat is found on the breast, far more than in any other type of poultry, and the thighs provide almost 25 percent. The breast meat contains approximately 25 percent protein and 2.5 percent fat. It has an exceptionally low water content and therefore must be barded and basted to prevent it from drying out. A quail prepared for roasting or broiling weighs around 4 ounces, and two birds are usually considered a single portion. This is one type of poultry in which the quality difference between fresh and frozen birds is considerable, and fresh birds are clearly preferable.

Ready for cooking. This is how quail are generally sold. They may be sold individually, but for the wholesale trade, they are generally sold in packages of six or twelve.

Squab
Columbae

Squab are, in fact, young pigeons. Around 300 species of pigeon, a member of the Columbae family, are found throughout the world. Pigeons have been known and used in a number of ways by people since the earliest times. In ancient China, for example, carrier pigeons were sent to and from Peking (Beijing) with important news. The Greeks, Romans, and Egyptians used pigeons for ritual sacrifice, and regarded them as oracles and messengers of the gods. The pigeon or dove is considered a holy bird, the embodiment of fertility and peace, by many peoples, and in Christianity it is the symbol of the Holy Spirit.

A distinction is generally drawn between wild pigeons (*Columba livia*) and domestic pigeons (*Columba livia domestica*). The latter are all descended from the wild rock pigeon (*Columba livia livia*), which is widespread in Europe, in the south as far as North Africa and in the east as far as the Caucasus. Blue, black, red, yellow, and white are the most common colors of its plumage. The dominant color is varying shades of blue. The eyes are red, brown-black or pearl-white, and the wing bands are mostly black. The faithful, monogamous pigeons nest in caves and in the dark areas of buildings and other masonry. The eggs are incubated by both the male and the female. Pigeons are robust, insensitive to temperature and undemanding.

Squabs, the nestlings of pigeons, are bred for their meat yield. The objective of the breeding is to produce as many saleable young as possible each year. A pair of pigeons will deposit a maximum of one to two eggs every thirty days. Therefore, each pair of pigeons will produce up to twenty-four squab a year. The most important meat squabs include the White King, which at almost 2 pounds, is one of the heaviest breeds and has a meaty breast; the Texan pigeon, which, at up to 1¾ pounds, is also rather heavy, with a broad meaty breast; the Carneau from southern Belgium and northern France, weighing up to 1½ pounds; the Mondain, from France, a heavyweight meat squab weighing up to 2 pounds; the Strasser, native to Austria, which is not very fertile, but weighs almost 2 pounds; and the Coburg lark, weighing up to 1¾ pounds, which has a broad, meaty breast.

Squabs are commonly reared in volaries and coops, especially in America, Italy, France, and Hungary. Between twenty and thirty pairs are kept in a volary, and there is space for ten to twenty volaries in a coop. The squabs remain in the nest

after hatching for twenty-eight days, when they have reached the ideal size for market. Up to that time they are "cropped"; that is, they are fed with pigeon milk, a secretion of the lining of the crop, by the parents.

A squab has about 26 percent breast meat and 10 percent leg meat. The live weight of squabs reaches 10 ounces to 1⅓ pounds, and the oven-ready birds weigh between 8 and 14 ounces. Nowadays most squabs are plucked mechanically; but they can also be plucked by hand. They are gutted like other poultry but have no gall bladder.

Squab meat is tender, delicious, digestible, and prized by gourmets because of its very powerful flavor. Young fattening birds should be roasted or prepared in a fricassee. Older pigeons should be boiled, steamed, or braised; they make an excellent soup and good forcemeat.

This is how squabs are sold. The ends of the wings are folded away on the back, and the neck is tucked in underneath. This gives the carcass a compact appearance.

Guinea fowl in an outdoor paddock (top) and in a closed coop (above), where chaff and wood shavings are used as litter. A well-balanced feed ensures good growth and high laying capacity.

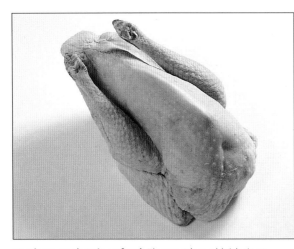

Ready-to-cook guinea fowl. The meat has a bluish tinge. Unlike a young fattening chicken, this bird lacks the clearly visible fat deposits and the fully fleshed muscles. Almost all recipes for roast pheasant, in particular for the breasts, can be used for young guinea fowl.

Guinea fowl
Numidinae

The guinea fowl belongs to the pheasant subfamily (Phasanidae). It comes originally from Africa, which is why it is sometimes also known as the African chicken. It was domesticated in Greece as far back as the fourth century BC, and it has been reared for centuries in Europe, particularly in France and Italy, and America as an ornamental and economically useful bird.

The original and still most common form of the domestic guinea fowl is the helmet guinea fowl (*Numida meleagris*). It has a roundish body, short wings and smooth, tightly packed blue-green plumage, which is studded all over with small white spots; this feature has led to its being called the "pearl hen" in Germany. Its most striking features are the bare face and the almost featherless neck. Instead of a comb, guinea fowl have a triangular red or corn-colored helmet on the top of the head. The wattle is reddish, the tail is short and pendulous, and the slate-gray legs lack a spur. Guinea fowl are lively animals, adaptable, undemanding, yet timid and easily frightened. Their penetrating, trumpet-like cry is unbearable.

As breeding animals, guinea fowl are reared predominantly in cages. Each hen will produce around 170 eggs or 115 chicks. At the age of six weeks, guinea fowl reach a weight of 1–1¼ pounds. They are then sold as single-portion birds and are readily used as a substitute for partridge. After a further six weeks they weigh about 2¾ pounds, and when fully grown, 3¾–4¼ pounds.

Guinea fowl provides 32 percent breast meat and 29 percent leg meat, the highest yield of these valuable parts after quail and turkey. They have the lowest fat content of all types of poultry, ranging from 1.1 percent in breast meat to 2.7 percent in the leg, and the highest protein content, at 25.2 percent in breast meat and 21.4 percent in the leg. The dark meat of the guinea fowl is tender, juicy, and reminiscent of the taste of pheasant. Only young birds are suitable for roasting. They should be barded and protected against drying out by frequent basting. Older animals, especially fat hens, should be braised or steamed.

Turkey

Meliagrididae

The turkey (*Meleagris gallopavo*), the largest and heaviest species of domestic poultry was found originally in Mexico, in the southwest, midwest and east of what became the United States, and as far north as Ontario. The conquistadors took the tamed wild turkeys from Mexico to Spain in 1520, from where they spread to other parts of Europe. Early English colonists brought some with them to America, where they were bred with native wild turkeys, producing the foundation stock of the modern American breeds.

Turkeys are large, long-legged birds. They have a powerful body which drops away to the tail, a broad breast, and a featherless, warty head. Fully grown males — usually called toms, stags or gobblers — have a tuft of black hair on the breast, while hens have a nipple. Turkeys are distinguished on the basis of color and weight. The major colors are bronze (background color black, with a bright bronze sheen, shimmering), white (white all over), and black (black all over and shimmering like velvet). The most popular large American turkeys are the Broad-Breasted Bronze, the Broad-Breasted White and the White Holland, while the Beltsville Small White is the most popular of the smaller breeds. Turkeys are classed on the basis of weight as light (oven-ready 7½–11 pounds), medium (oven-ready 12–21 pounds) and heavy (oven-ready 22–27 pounds), and very heavy (up to 40 pounds).

Toms are sexually mature at thirty-one weeks; hens at between thirty and thirty-two weeks. The hens lay eggs almost all year around, producing a total of around 150 eggs with a weight of 2½–3 ounces per egg. There are many small turkey breeders who still use outdoor, or free-range, methods of rearing, but the large worldwide supply comes from a relatively few intensive producers who rear turkeys indoors, mainly with ground management, although lighter birds can be reared in cages. Criteria for breeding are early maturity, rapid growth, hardiness, the highest possible meat content, and the lowest possible bone content. The heavy white broad-breasted hybrid (from White and Beltsville turkeys) fulfills these requirements best. Turkeys are brought to market before they are sexually mature: hens of eight to twelve weeks and up to 11 pounds live weight are sold whole. Hens of fifteen to eighteen

The large toms, such as this hybrid, have a big, broad breast, which is considerably heavier than that of the turkey hen.

This strange-looking bird has a number of distinctive features. Particularly striking is the tuft of black hair, which feels like horsehair, on the breast of the adult tom.

Hens of hybrid origin. As with all intensive breeding, the objectives are rapid growth, the highest possible meat content, and the lowest possible bone weight.

These farmyard turkeys in a Mexican market have a much smaller breast and more muscular flesh than intensively reared hybrids.

weeks and 15–20 pounds, and toms of twenty to twenty-four weeks and 30–37 pounds live weight are usually sold in portions.

The turkey provides a range of meat of different colors and consistencies. The legs have a dark, firm flesh. The breast meat is particularly lean, tender, and white, while the meat around the neck and on the sides is fattier. Turkey meat is very popular because it is not only very tasty but also very nutritious. The high proportion of protein (24 percent in breast meat, 21 percent in thigh meat) is rich in essential amino acids. The low proportion of fat (2 percent in breast meat, 8 percent in thigh meat — and less if the skin is removed) is rich in valuable polyunsaturated fatty acids.

Turkey is also a good source of zinc, and provides phosphorus, potassium, magnesium, and, in the dark meat, significant amounts of iron. An average serving of turkey supplies the daily requirements of vitamin B_{12}, and nearly half the daily requirement of niacin.

Turkey is sold as a whole carcass (fresh or frozen), as portions (breast, thigh, drumstick, wing), as turkey meat (scallops, rolls, and roasts) and as processed products. While the portions and deep-frozen whole birds are sold all year around, fresh whole carcasses are sold mainly from September to March, especially in time for Thanksgiving and Christmas.

Light turkeys, also called baby or broiler turkeys, and medium turkeys are roasted whole, and can be prepared in the same way as chicken, with or without stuffing. Older turkeys are used in soups and stews.

This turkey hen weighs about 13 pounds and is ideal for roasting whole. The bird on the opposite page is a tom weighing about 30 pounds, and is better cut into individual portions.

Cutting turkey into individual pieces

Large, heavy turkeys are now seldom roasted whole at home, and it may even be difficult to find large, heavy portions. However, if you find a source of fresh turkeys, you can buy a large bird and cut it into portions as shown in the picture sequence on the opposite page, for which a 30-pound tom turkey was used.

Table 6 shows the average range of weights for whole turkeys and turkey portions of a medium-weight bird. As can be seen, the popular breast, leg, and wing make up around half of the total carcass weight. In comparison, the breast portion of the bird in the picture sequence opposite weighed 9½ pounds, close to a third of the total weight ; the legs weighed 3¾ pounds (thighs 2¼ pounds, drumsticks 1½ pounds), and the whole wings 1½ pounds.

Table 5: Average weight of turkeys and turkey portions	
Whole turkeys	
Heavy turkeys	depending on age, between 13 and 33 pounds
Medium turkeys	depending on age, between 9 and 22 pounds
Small turkeys	depending on age, between 6½ and 15 pounds
Turkey portions	
Whole turkey breast:	2–6½ lb
Turkey leg	2–3 lb
Thigh	1–1½ lb
Lower leg	8–14 oz
Turkey wing	7–12 oz

1 Loosen the wing and splay it out. Feel for the shoulder joint, cut through it and remove the wing.

2 Remove the lower wing, feeling and cutting through the joint connecting it with the middle section.

3 Separate the middle wing from the upper wing, feeling the joint and cutting through the middle of it.

Plucking a turkey by hand.

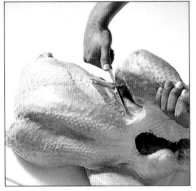

4 Loosen the leg, lift slightly, and splay out. Cut through the skin between the body and the leg.

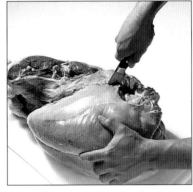

5 Cut down right through to the hip joint. Push the leg away from the body and remove.

6 Separate the drumstick from the thigh, making a straight cut through the joint.

7 Grip the breast firmly and pull off the skin, starting at the tip of the breast. Remove remaining visible fat.

8 Turn the carcass onto its side. Cut through the ribs on either side following the line of the connective tissue.

9 Lay it on its back again. Hold the back firmly. Grip the tip of the breast and pull it hard away from the back.

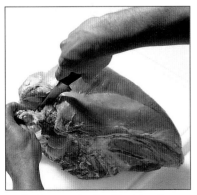

10 Remove the shoulder joints from the separated breast portion on both sides up to the start of the neck.

11 Carefully cut along between the ribs and the meat, and remove the breast from the carcass.

12 Using a sharp knife, carefully remove the fillet from the thick end of the breast.

Stark contrasts in color characterize the different types of meat in the turkey. The light breast meat is more tender than the dark, strong leg meat.

To make scallops: Work from the middle of the breast to the tip, cutting diagonally into slices.

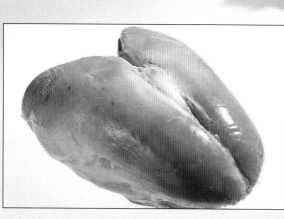

Turkey breast: One of the finest cuts of the turkey, this tender white meat is very low in fat.

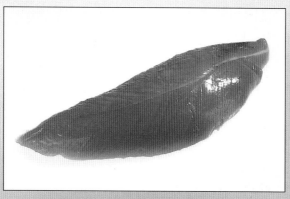

Turkey fillets are cut from the small breast muscle and are particularly suitable for medallions.

Turkey scallops are cut from the large breast muscle, and can be used like veal. The tips are excellent for ragout.

The parts of the turkey

There seem to be no limits to the culinary uses of turkey meat. A whole bird yields a large amount of meat, which can be prepared as individual cuts or used in prepared products. The individual parts such as the breast, thigh, drumstick, and wing do differ markedly in color and taste. The light, tender breast meat can be compared to veal. The darker, stronger leg meat has a very slightly gamey taste. As scallops, steak, fillet, or a rolled roast, turkey breast can be prepared in many ways. The legs are most suited to roasting, and the drumsticks are also good when braised. The wings can be used to make soup, or for broiling and braising. Ready-to-cook products range from fillets, scallops or steaks, sometimes coated in breadcrumbs, as *cordon bleu* products, to rolled roasts, kebabs, meatballs, and strips. Slices of roast and smoked turkey are popular sandwich fillings and delicatessen products.

The whole wing can weigh up to ¾ pound. During cutting, separate and remove the sinews in the joints.

Upper, middle and lower wing sections; the amount of meat on each piece varies.

The middle wings are often used for frying, barbecuing, and broiling after the bone has been removed.

Whole leg The strong, dark meat is very popular. The leg can be separated into the thigh and the drumstick.

The thigh is most suitable for rolled roasts and for stuffing after the bone has been removed.

The drumstick can be roasted whole. For best results, carefully remove the tough sinews at the lower end first.

Diced meat from the breast (rear) and thigh (foreground).

Strips are very versatile. Strips of breast meat are particularly tender.

A rolled roast can be made from breast meat or boned thigh.

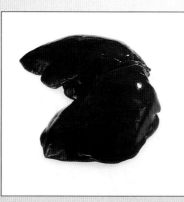

The liver may weigh up to 5 ounces. Its strong flavor comes out best when roasted.

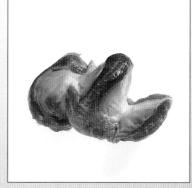

The gizzard can be used in stews after removing the leathery skin. It is also used in making stock and gravy.

The heart can be roasted or used in stews and sauces after removing the large blood vessels and washing thoroughly.

Duck eggs are larger and richer in flavor than hen's eggs, for which they may be substituted in any dish not requiring careful measurement.

These free-range muscovy ducks have muscular flesh and a particularly strong taste.

In China, ducks are raised in the rice fields. They walk on the small dikes between the fields and find plenty to eat in the marshy ground.

Duck
Anatinae

Ducks are dabbling or diving fowl of various sizes and breeds. Dabbling ducks obtain their food from the surface of the water and by tipping tail-end up to eat vegetation below the surface in shallow water; on land, they have a horizontal posture, as they do on the water. Diving ducks, as their name indicates, dive below the surface of the water to find their food, and on land have a more vertical posture. The original form of all domestic ducks is the mallard (*Anas platyrhynchos*), a dabbling duck with gray-brown game-colored plumage. The drake has a shimmering dark-green head and neck, a white collar and the well-known drake's lock on the tail. Mallards are found throughout Europe, North Africa, North America, and northern Asia.

Ducks have been kept and cooked for more than 2,300 years in China, and were domesticated as long ago as 1000 BC in Greece. Today several major breeds of domestic duck, which may be as much as three times the size of their wild relations, are reared for their meat. The Aylesbury duck, which is a pure white bird originating in England, is a large, heavy duck with a full breast and tender, very flavorful meat, with a live weight of 6–7¾ pounds, producing around 80 eggs, of nearly 3 ounces each, per year. The Rouen duck, a beautiful large bird originally from Normandy, is wide and its body almost touches the ground. It is a heavy meat duck with a live weight of 8½ –11 pounds, producing around 60 to 90 eggs of about 3 ounces each per year. Its distinctive feature is that it is not killed in the usual manner, but suffocated, so that the blood remains in the body. The meat is reddish and very fine. The Nantes, or Nantais, duck is a smaller, leaner bird, which, even if well fattened, weighs no more than 4½ pounds after four months. The Pekin, or Peking, duck is an easy-to-fatten duck, which lays well. The White Pekin duck, a pure white bird descended from white ducks brought to the United States from China in 1873, is favored in North America, accounting for 60 percent of ducks raised for the table. They reach a market weight of 7 pounds in eight weeks, and have a good meat yield. Wild ducks, which may be available during the hunting season, are less fatty and taste gamier than the domestic varieties.

Muscovy ducks are native to Central and tropical South America. Zoologically, they come between the duck and the goose, and belong to the genus *Cairina*. They are particularly robust birds. In the wild they live on rivers in woodlands and sleep and nest in trees. They have no voice, and can only hiss. Domestic muscovys have gray, white, or speckled plumage, and a bare, red face. The body and tail are longer than those of the mallard. The drake reaches a weight of 8½ pounds in eleven weeks, while the duck reaches only 5½ pounds in ten weeks, both producing a high proportion of meat, which is considered a delicacy, and relatively little fat.

Ducks are lively, undemanding animals that are easy to keep and therefore are particularly suitable for intensive fattening. Commercially, they provide us with eggs, meat, and feathers or down (up to 10½ ounces per fully grown duck). In France, they also provide the *foie gras* obtained from force-feeding, as in geese.

The ducks of the greatest commercial importance are the meat ducks, and of these, the White Pekin and the muscovy are the leaders. Probably the largest duck farm in the world is that run by the Cherry Valley company in England, where several lines are bred. The oldest and best-known area for duck breeding, however, is on Long Island, where the first White Pekin ducks were raised.

The majority of the ducks sold — fresh and frozen — are really ducklings six to eight weeks old. The timing of bringing the birds to market is based on the first molt, as immediately prior to this they are particularly easy to pluck. With mechanical dry plucking the feathers can be removed in good condition, but wet plucking requires less work. In both processes the down is removed in an adjacent wax immersing bath.

Ducks have a large skeleton and thus a relatively high proportion of bone. As the fat content is also rather high, the meat yield is correspondingly lower. Pekin duck has 27 percent breast and 23 percent leg meat, and muscovy duck has nearly 25 percent breast meat and 28 percent leg meat. Duck meat generally contains around 20 percent protein and up to 6 percent fat.

When buying duck, look for fleshy, not-too-fat animals with a light skin. Before cooking, remove all visible fat. Ducklings are then best roasted in the oven on a rack so that as much as possible of the remaining fat can drip down. Older or less tender ducks benefit from being braised. Duck breast is also ideal for cooking in individual portions.

Dry plucking is laborious, but good for the feathers and for the cook, as the skin is crispier when cooked.

With hot wax, even the smallest feathers are removed. This method is gentler than blanching in boiling water.

To cut a duck into individual pieces:

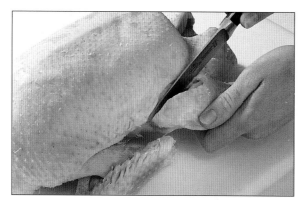

1 First remove the legs: cut into the skin between the body and the leg, pulling the leg somewhat away from the body.

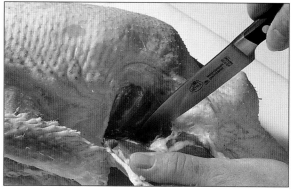

2 In one hand, hold the leg away from the body. Using a sharp knife, cut down along the carcass to the hip joint.

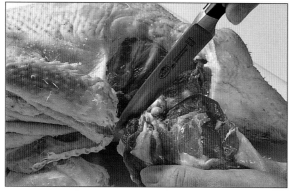

3 Bend the hip joint apart and sever it, carefully cutting through the sinews and the flesh. Remove the other leg in the same way.

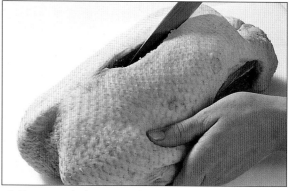

4 To remove the breast, cut along the breastbone with a sharp knife, then loosen the breast to the right and left as far as the cartilage of the ribcage.

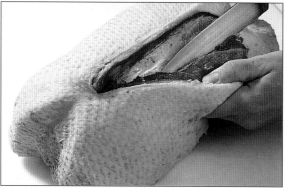

5 Working along the breastplate, hold the meat away from the carcass with the hand, and scrape it off the bone piece by piece with a sharp knife.

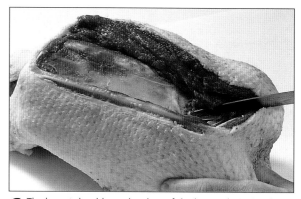

6 The breast should now be clear of the breastplate. Continue to work carefully to separate the meat from the carcass along the wishbone.

7 Pull the breast from the carcass with one hand and remove it in one piece by cutting carefully along the carcass.

8 The four separate parts of the duck — 2 breasts and 2 legs — and the rest of the carcass with the wings still attached.

Stuffing and trussing
Using duck as an example

Stuffings are more than just an ideal accompaniment for poultry. They also give the surrounding meat additional flavor and an attractive full shape. Whether the stuffing contains bread, chestnuts, or forcemeat, the technique is the same. Sewing up the opening prevents the stuffing from leaking out during cooking, and helps to preserve the attractive shape of the bird.

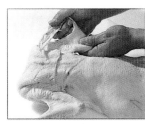

To truss a duck:

Lay the duck on its breast and push the tips of the wings under the second wing joint. Fold the neck skin onto the back.

Push a trussing needle through both parts of the wing, the neck skin, under the backbone, and through the other wing.

To stuff a duck:

Prepare the duck for roasting. Using the fingers, loosen any fat still in the abdominal cavity and remove it carefully.

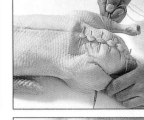

Turn the duck over and push the needle through the drumstick so that it comes out through the other leg.

Spoon the stuffing into the cavity and spread it evenly. Do not fill the cavity completely, as the stuffing will expand during cooking.

Tie the ends of the kitchen string together securely. The legs should point horizontally to the rear, and the duck should lie flat on the board.

To close the opening, press the ends of the skin together with the thumb and index finger, and secure with toothpicks or skewers.

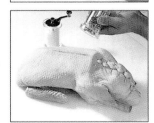

Season the stuffed duck with salt and freshly ground pepper, and rub in evenly.

Bind the skewers from top to bottom with kitchen string, crossing it over between each skewer, and tie a knot at the end.

1 Pull the neck skin back over the carcass, expose the wishbone, and gently loosen the skin on the bone.

Boning a whole bird

Two methods, using duck as an example

To stuff a whole bird and avoid any loss when carving, you must hollow out the carcass; that is, completely remove all the bones except for those in the wings and legs. For a galantine, however, you must remove even these limb bones. In both methods — hollowing out on this page, and boning for a galantine on the opposite page — the wing tips are removed at the elbow joint and the feet are removed at the knee joint. Sufficient skin is left on at the neck end so that you can sew up the stuffed bird or roll the galantine neatly.

2 Twist and remove the wishbone, and push the skin down gently toward the shoulder joints.

3 Feel to locate the shoulder joints, uncover and sever them, twisting the joint slightly.

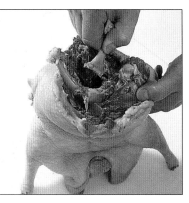

4 Remove the meat from the collarbones. Separate the collarbones from the breastbone by pressing lightly.

5 Carefully pull the collarbones away from the shoulder blade without tearing the flesh.

6 Working from the shoulder, pull the meat away along the carcass and separate it from the hip joint.

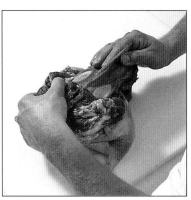

7 Turn the duck around and gently but firmly pull the breast meat away from the carcass.

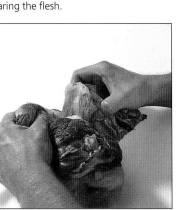

8 Uncover the backbone as far as the rump. Remove the breastbone by pulling gently.

9 Cut off the rump with the carcass so that there are 3–4 vertebrae remaining in the flesh.

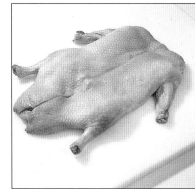

10 Only the leg bones and wing bones now remain in the hollowed-out duck.

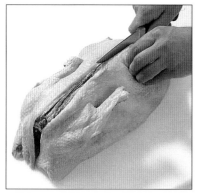

1 Make an incision on both sides of the backbone cutting down to the bone, and remove the skin.

2 Feel to locate the shoulder joint, uncover and sever it, twisting the joint slightly.

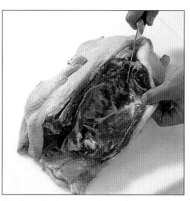

3 Detach the meat along the carcass as far as the hip joint. Feel for the hip joint, uncover and sever it.

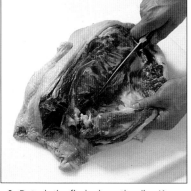

4 Detach the flesh along the ribs. Keep the blade of the knife always pointed toward the carcass.

5 Be careful not to damage the breast when cutting along the breastbone. Detach the other breast in the same way.

6 Keeping the carcass clear, loosen the breastbone from the skin. Do not damage the skin.

7 Cut around the stumps of the wing bones, scrape them clean and remove, pushing the meat in.

8 In the same way, remove the remaining pieces of leg bone and push the meat in.

9 Pull out the severed sinews in the wings and the legs with a small pair of flat-nosed pliers or tweezers.

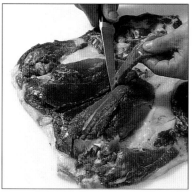

10 Remove visible pads of fat. Even up the edges of the skin. Remove the small breast fillets.

11 Slice open the breasts and fold them outward. Lay the small breast fillets on the bare lower sections.

12 The duck skin must be covered all over with an equal amount of meat in order to cook evenly.

Goose

Anseriformes

The original form of the domestic goose is the common wild goose, or graylag (*Anser anser*), which is native to Europe. It was domesticated by the ancient Germans and kept because of its excellent meat, its fat and its feathers. Geese are widespread and of great economic importance in Eastern Europe. There are, of course, many species of wild geese in North America — the familiar Canada goose (*Branta canadensis*), the barnacle (*B. leucopsis*), the brant (*B. bernicla*), and the snow goose (*B. coerulescens*) — but the domestic goose is not commercially bred or reared on anywhere near the same scale as the more popular chicken and turkey.

In the wild, geese are monogamous birds, which live their whole lives in couples. They live in herds, and are sensitive and affectionate. They can also be quite vicious when they are on the attack. (Their vigilance was valued by the ancient Romans, for it is well known that the geese saved the Capitol when it came under threat from the Gauls.) The goose and the gander are similar in appearance. They are sexually mature after ten to twelve months, and the geese lay around 50 to 60 eggs between the beginning of February and the end of May.

Magnificent snow-white geese. Many small breeders have taken up the natural rearing of this attractive bird.

The swan goose (*Anser cygnoides*), of eastern Asia, has also been domesticated in the West.

Commercially, the two most important domestic breeds of geese are the Emden, or Embden, and the Toulouse. The Emden is a completely white, large, heavy but nonetheless agile breed with a broad breast and a broad back. The Toulouse is a gray, very heavy, slow-moving breed with a box-shaped rump and a thick neck, and traditionally has been bred for its fatty liver (*foie gras*). The Emden-Toulouse cross is a popular hybrid. Other breeds include the heavy Pomeranian goose, and the light, very fertile swan goose, which is notable for the bulge on its forehead and its trumpet-like cry. Geese lay about 50 eggs, each weighing about 5½ ounces, a year. They are often plucked live for their feathers, which appears to have no effect on their laying or meat yield.

The time it takes to rear geese to their market weight depends on the way in which they are kept. With rapid fattening, the birds reach an average final weight of 9½–14 pounds after a good nine weeks. With intensive rearing, geese may reach a weight of 12–14 pounds after fifteen to sixteen weeks, while birds that are pasture farmed weigh 14–17½ pounds after twenty to thirty-two weeks.

Geese are not feed for the twelve hours immediately before slaughter. To preserve the quality of the feathers, the still warm animals are dry-plucked mechanically and the down is removed in an adjacent wax immersing bath. A goose has a dressed, or oven-ready, weight that is 72–75 percent of its live weight. So a live bird weighing around 12 pounds will have an oven-ready weight of about 8¾ pounds, while a 20-pound goose may have an oven-ready weight of 15 pounds. The goose has the highest proportion of fat of all types of poultry. Rendered to a pure white, it is prized by chefs and other cooks, particularly for frying potatoes.

Geese are sold fresh or frozen. The main season for fresh goose is the winter months. The birds should appear uniformly pale, should have no remains of feathers or tears in the skin, and should have a fat skin and a fleshy breast. Early fattening geese are slaughtered before the first mature plumage. The projection of the breastbone is flexible. When ready to cook, they weigh around 9 pounds. Young geese are slaughtered after the first mature plumage. The projection of the breastbone is still flexible. When ready to cook, they weigh 11–15 pounds, and account for the largest proportion of those sold. Geese over one year old are slaughtered after the laying period, by which time the projection of the breast bone is ossified. They are seldom sold, since goose meat is really palatable only during the first year.

Goose is usually roasted to bring out its full flavor; more rarely, it is braised, boiled, or steamed. As the

These geese in the Périgord region of France are bred primarily to obtain as large a liver as possible. Nonetheless, their meat has a good flavor, and is mostly made into the confit that is typical of the region. This meat cooked in its own fat is a traditional ingredient for the famous cassoulet.

goose is a very fat bird, it is important to remove all visible fat before cooking; render this valuable substance and use it to enhance the flavor of other dishes. Roast the goose on a rack so that the fat in the meat can drip down.

Popular products made from goose include smoked goose breast, goose liver pâté (*pâté de foie gras*), confit (preserved goose meat), and goose liver sausage. *Foie gras* is also used as an ingredient in game pâté and terrines. The major suppliers of the much sought-after *foie gras* are France, Italy, Hungary, and Israel. Force-feeding of geese is prohibited in some countries on grounds of animal welfare.

After intensive rearing lasting around fifteen weeks, the geese weigh between 10 and 12 lb. Pasture reared birds are fattened for up to thirty weeks. In spite of this the birds are then only 2–4 lb heavier.

Smoked chicken, lean
and with a delicate flavor, is
a delicious topping for toast
and pizza, as the meat goes well
with tomato and cheese.

Good, solid smoked leg of goose. Under
the fatty skin is delicate meat, which tastes
delicious on rye bread with horseradish sauce.

A range of smoked products

A *substitute for ham*

In many countries there is a tradition of smoking
the fat waterfowl, and there is a range of different
recipes and techniques for doing so. But lean poultry, such as chicken and turkey, can also be smoked
and can be used in many different ways in cooking

as a substitute for ham. The drumsticks of the
turkey, with their dark meat, have a particularly delicious, strong flavor when smoked. Both the lean and
the fat meat of duck and goose are wonderful smoked,
and can be used in a variety of ways in hot dishes.

The meaty turkey drumstick, although it has sinews running through it, has a much stronger flavor when smoked than the extremely lean, fine breast meat. It is particularly tasty heated through in a pot of sauerkraut and served with caraway potatoes — a good example of appetizing, low-fat cuisine.

Smoked breast of goose: two breasts are put together and smoked. Do not cut too thin.

Smoked breast of Pekin duck with a very thin covering of fat. The firm meat can be cut thin.

Smoked duck breast as prepared in Spain. The meat is very strongly spiced, so even the fat is flavorful.

Smoked breast of muscovy duck as prepared in France. The meat is firm and the coating of fat is spicy.

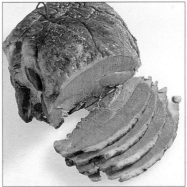

Smoked turkey thigh with a light covering of fat. A strong-flavored meat that can be eaten hot or cold.

This smoked turkey roll is extremely lean and can be cut thin for use in sandwiches and salads.

Smoked rolled turkey that even looks like ham and can be used instead of ham in hot dishes.

Smoked rolled poultry roast made with chicken or turkey. The spicy skin makes it a fine cold roast.

A huge variety of fresh sausages are made from poultry. They are similar in name and in seasoning to the traditional range of sausages made from pork and beef. In most cases, they have a lower fat content, except for the salami, which has to be made with the addition of pork fat.

Poultry sausage is suitable for sandwiches and simple salads, since it goes well with other flavors.

Poultry loaf can be cubed or cut into thick slices. Try it fried in butter, with eggs and chives.

Chicken roulade is made with finely spiced chicken breast. It is delicious with onions and a vinaigrette dressing.

Turkey ham, made from the breast meat, is slightly smoked and seasoned, contains only 2 percent fat.

Chicken in aspic — roughly chopped meat in a spicy gelatin — is lean and refreshing.

Chicken roll with green pepper made with breast meat is strongly spiced.

Sausages made from poultry meat
Delicious low-fat food

This variety of sausage products made exclusively or predominantly from poultry meat is the equal in taste to those made from other meats. Products similar to all common types of fresh sausage and smoked sausage can be found in this lean range. The meat comes only from lean types of poultry, such as chicken and, especially, turkey, which can provide large pieces of meat.

Sausages for frying and boiling. They may look the same as pork sausages, knackwurst, and frankfurters, but these sausages are all made from poultry meats.

Poultry liver sausage has the fine taste of poultry liver and a soft spreading consistency.

Stocks, soups, and sauces

Stock is indispensable in cooking, an essential basis for soups and sauces. Among the various stocks, poultry stock — fond de volaille— is preeminent. It is made from poultry meat, especially the less good parts – such as the neck, wings, gizzard, and carcass — with the addition of calves' feet or veal bones. Chicken stock — fond de poulet — is, as its name indicates, made with chicken rather than any other poultry, and is essential wherever a good broth is required. Fond de poulet is made in different concentrations depending on how it is to be used. Fond blanc de volaille is the basic light stock, the ideal ingredient for light meat, poultry, and vegetable dishes, it can even be used in cooking fish. When it is somewhat more concentrated, it becomes the popular chicken bouillon, which, in turn, is the basis of many poultry and vegetable soups. Reduced even further and clarified with egg white, it becomes consommé. The most concentrated form of chicken stock is glace de volaille, which is made by boiling the stock for several hours to reduce it to around one-tenth or less of its original volume. Such a concentrate is the ideal ingredient wherever a lot of flavor is required, not only in poultry, but also in other meat, game, and vegetable dishes, for in spite of its stronger flavor glace de volaille is still so neutral that it does not mask the flavors of the other ingredients.

It is possible to vary the taste of a stock or bouillon with suitable vegetables.

1 Using a sharp knife, carefully remove as much fat as possible from the carcasses.

2 Using a small chopper or a large knife, chop the carcasses into pieces of equal size.

3 Rinse the hearts and gizzards under running water and cut them into pieces of similar size.

4 Heat the oil in a roasting pan in the oven, and roast the carcasses and giblets until well browned.

5 Add the diced vegetables, onion, peppercorns, and garlic, and continue to cook.

6 As soon as the vegetables are lightly colored, add the tomato paste and stir once or twice.

7 Pour some water onto the dry-roasted mixture, turning and mixing it thoroughly.

8 Continue to add water in stages and reduce until the mixture has acquired the desired color.

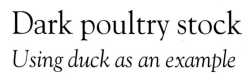

Dark poultry stock
Using duck as an example

The key to achieving perfect flavor in sauces lies in the basic stock used. The finer and more aromatic the stock is, the better the sauce will be. Dark stock is the basis for dark sauces. It can be made using all the trimmings of a duck: the carcass (the skeleton without the skin), the giblets, neck, and wings. It acquires its color from roasting all the ingredients first. It is seasoned only very sparingly, and is not salted at all, as it will be reduced for use in sauces and glazes.

When you make this stock, use only a single type of poultry, for mixing in parts of other animals will adulterate the typical taste of the poultry. You can make a dark poultry stock of chicken, guinea fowl, or turkey using the recipe on these pages without changing the other ingredients.

9 Add water until all the ingredients are completely covered, then add parsley. Simmer for 3–4 hours.

10 Carefully pour the contents of the roasting pan into a large pot.

Makes 2½ quarts

2 duck carcasses, with necks, about 5 lb
2 duck hearts, 2 duck gizzards
¼ cup oil
⅔ cup chopped carrots
1 cup chopped celeriac, 1 cup chopped leek
1 onion, halved and studded with 1 clove
10 black peppercorns
½ garlic clove with skin
1 tablespoon tomato paste
13 cups water
fresh flat-leaf parsley, 1 bay leaf
bouquet garni: thyme, celery leaves, and sage

A good stock has a low fat content. Remove all the visible fat from the carcasses before using them. Carefully skim off the fat that collects on the surface with the proteins in the form of foam when the stock is being boiled. To make a clear stock, it is important to strain the liquid to remove any sediment. After that, reduce the stock to the desired consistency, remove the fat again, pour into portion-sized containers as required, and cool.

11 Bring to the boil briefly, removing the foam frequently with a spoon.

12 Add the bouquet garni and cook for a further 3–4 hours.

13 Line a conical strainer with cheesecloth and carefully strain the stock.

14 Use a spoon to remove the fat that comes to the surface as the stock cools.

LIGHT POULTRY STOCK MADE WITH CHICKEN CARCASSES

The method is similar to that used for the dark stock on pages 50–1, but the carcasses must not be allowed to color. You can also make this stock with the carcasses of other types of poultry, such as duck or goose.

Makes 2½ quarts

4½ lb chicken carcasses, with neck, gizzard, and heart
1½ lb chopped veal bones
¼ cup vegetable oil
¾ cup chopped carrots
¾ cup chopped celery
¾ cup chopped leek
¼ cup chopped celeriac
1 cup dry white wine, 13 cups water
1 bay leaf, 15 peppercorns
4 whole allspice
1 garlic clove, lightly crushed

CHICKEN BROTH MADE WITH A WHOLE CHICKEN

The general term "broth" means a full-bodied, clear, light bouillon. Unlike a stock, it takes its strength not only from the bones but also from the meat, which is cooked with it. It is very easy to make, and it serves a dual purpose: the broth is the basis for soups and sauces, while the meat cooked with it can be used for ragouts, salads, or garnishes. It is best to use a whole boiling fowl to make chicken broth. Such a bird gives off a lot of fat, but this can be skimmed off while cooking or removed from the cooled broth later. To give the broth a beautiful deep color, add a couple of onions roasted in their skins.

Makes 3 quarts

1 boiling fowl, 4½–5½ lb, quartered
2 lb chopped veal bones
17 cups water
20 peppercorns
2 garlic cloves, lightly crushed
1 onion studded with 4 cloves
For the bouquet garni:
1 carrot, ½ leek, 1 celery stalk
2 bay leaves, 2 sprigs fresh thyme
6 sprigs fresh parsley

Rinse the chopped carcasses and the veal bones under running water for 30 minutes. Allow to drain thoroughly. Heat the oil in a roasting pan, lightly fry the carcasses and veal bones, add the roughly chopped vegetables and continue to cook, without allowing the ingredients to color. Add the wine. Transfer to a pot, add the water and bring to the boil once. Skim and simmer gently for 2 hours, adding more water if necessary. After 1 hour add the herbs and spices. At the end of the cooking time, leave to infuse for 20 minutes, then strain through a cheesecloth.

Cover the boiling fowl and the veal bones with hot water and bring to a boil as quickly as possible. Allow to boil until foam collects on the surface. Drain and rinse with warm water. Cover with fresh water, return to the boil and again skim carefully. Reduce the heat and simmer for 3 hours. After 2 hours, add the herbs, spices, onion, and bouquet garni, and, if necessary, more water. Strain the finished broth through a cheesecloth, allow to cool, and skim off the fat.

Poultry stock

The basis of good poultry cooking

Whether you call it poultry stock, poultry broth, or bouillon, what is meant is a light, full-strength broth that can be used as soup or as a basis for sauces, or for poaching poultry and making galantines. It can also be made into a strong consommé by clarifying it with meat (see pages 54–5). The two main ways to prepare a light broth are shown on the opposite page. The first method uses: poultry carcasses — in other words the bones and trimmings — and the second uses a whole bird; a boiling fowl will provide most flavor. A combination of poultry carcasses and boiling fowl is a very good third possibility, when it is cooked according to the bouillon method. The main ingredients then are: $1/2$ boiling fowl (approximately 3 lb), 2 lb poultry carcasses, and 2 lb of veal bones. Veal bones are used when making chicken broth because they refine the taste and provide a particularly large amount of jellying agents, which give the reduced stock a pleasant consistency.

The light stock or chicken broth is used for white sauces, fricassees, and blanquettes, and for poaching poultry; the dark stock is used to make brown sauces and dark ragouts, and for braising. Although the quantities of ingredients used in the recipes opposite seem at first glance to be very large, it is worth making the full recipe and storing any broth or stock you do not need immediately. Poured hot into glass jars and tightly sealed, it will keep for up to two weeks in the refrigerator and several months in the freezer. Stocks and broths are not salted so that they can be reduced as desired, enabling them to be used in a great many ways.

Poultry glaze

The optimum in taste

A glaze is a highly concentrated stock. Its basis is a strained poultry stock that is reduced very slowly until it covers the back of a spoon without running off. Mainly as a result of the proportion of veal bones or calves' feet used, this reduction becomes a firm jelly when cold. It can be kept in small portions for weeks in the refrigerator or in the freezer, an instantly available "flavor enhancer" that can be used not just for poultry, but also for other meat, and even fish, dishes.

POULTRY CONSOMMÉ

This example of poultry consommé is made with chicken broth, but you can use any poultry broth.

Makes 1½ quarts

¾ lb lean clarifying meat, such as beef shank
1 cup finely diced vegetables: celeriac, carrots, leek
1 cup crushed ice, 3 egg whites
1 garlic clove, lightly crushed
10 peppercorns, 1 sprig fresh thyme
10 sprigs fresh parsley
9 cups fully defatted chicken broth (see pages 52–3)
salt

Make the consommé as described in the picture sequence below. It is important to stir constantly while the clarifying meat is being heated to prevent the egg whites from burning on the bottom of the pot. When you stop stirring, the egg white will bind all the solid substances.

Pass the carefully prepared, fat-free clarifying meat through the coarse disk of a grinder.

Clarifying and completing the consommé:

Put the meat, vegetables, ice, and egg whites into a saucepan and mix well together.

Mix the spices into the ice-cold meat and vegetable mixture, then add the poultry broth.

Heat through, stirring continuously so that the egg white does not stick to the bottom of the pot.

As soon as the broth boils, stop stirring. Simmer for 30–40 minutes.

Remove from the heat, add salt, allow to rest for 10 minutes, then pour through a strainer lined with cheesecloth.

Consommé

A strongly flavored, clear liquid

A soup like this, which is as clear as glass and has so much flavor, cannot be made from poultry alone. However carefully a bouillon is prepared, such transparency can be achieved only by a separate clarification process. Egg white is the key to clarification, but it does not affect the taste of the soup. The flavor is enhanced markedly by using beef. This so-called "clarifying meat" has to be a completely lean cut, rich in sinews. Shank of beef is ideal because of its high protein content (around 20 percent) and the collagen in the sinews. To enhance the taste of poultry consommé even further, add lightly roasted poultry bones.

CONSOMMÉ OF GUINEA FOWL AND TOMATOES

This recipe is a good example of how the taste of a poultry consommé can be changed by the acidity of tomatoes.

Makes 1 quart
1 lb guinea fowl carcasses
½ lb lean clarifying meat, such as beef shank
½ cup finely diced vegetables: celeriac, carrots, celery
½ cup crushed ice
2 egg whites
½ cup tomato paste
2 cups diced fresh tomato
6 cups light broth of guinea fowl or chicken (see pages 52–3)
1 garlic clove, lightly crushed
10 peppercorns
2 fresh lovage leaves, 10 sprigs fresh parsley
salt

Chop the guinea fowl carcasses into small pieces, place them in a large pot, cover with water, and bring to a boil once over a high heat. Immediately pour into a strainer and drain well. Pass the clarifying meat through the coarse disk of a meat grinder, add to a clean saucepan with the prepared vegetables, the ice, and the egg whites, and mix well. Add the tomato paste and the diced tomato, and mix. Pour on the cold broth and bring to a boil, as

Vegetable strips are a suitable garnish for any consommé. Cooked meat from the appropriate type of poultry can also be used.

described in the picture sequence on the opposite page. Add the guinea fowl carcasses, herbs, and spices, and leave to infuse over a low heat for approximately 30 minutes. Remove from the heat,

add salt, and allow to stand for a further 10 minutes, then pour through a strainer lined with cheesecloth. Serve with a suitable garnish, such as diced tomato or guinea fowl meat.

Soup garnishes made from poultry meat

A delicious addition to consommés and cream soups

The usual soup garnishes, such as noodles, rice, and vegetables, can, of course, be used for all poultry soups. However, quenelles, gnocchi, or ravioli made from poultry meat are more distinctive in both taste and appearance, and are a splendid addition to soups if they are made from the same type of poultry as that used in the stock. These small, light forcemeats are not difficult to make, as the following recipes show, and they can be made from all types of poultry meat. Use different herbs and spices to vary the garnishes as desired.

Quenelles of poultry go particularly well with vegetable garnishes, as these rosettes of quail with turnips and zucchini show.

ROSETTES OF QUAIL

This decorative soup garnish can also be made in the form of quenelles or elongated gnocchi, but they look particularly attractive piped into rosettes. You can use pieces of meat that are not suitable for roasting or are simply not needed in another recipe. In the case of quails, for example, the legs are often left over, as some dishes require only the breasts.

Serves 4
5 oz quail meat
salt, freshly ground white pepper
pinch of ground ginger
2 teaspoons brandy
½ egg white, chilled
½ cup heavy cream, well-chilled or slightly frozen
1 cup light poultry stock (see pages 52–3)

Finely dice the quail meat, place it in a bowl, and sprinkle with pepper and ginger. Drizzle with brandy, cover, and chill thoroughly in the refrigerator. Mix finely in a mixer and add the egg white. Gradually work in the cream. Push the forcemeat through a fine strainer and chill again. Place in a pastry bag with a star-shaped tip, pipe rosettes onto a lightly oiled baking sheet, and freeze very slightly. Remove from the baking sheet with a knife and poach in simmering poultry stock — it must *not* boil — for 2–3 minutes before serving.

DUCK LIVER GNOCCHI

Any other poultry liver can be used for this recipe, but duck liver certainly makes the tastiest gnocchi.

Serves 4
3 oz lean duck meat without skin
¾ cup diced duck liver
salt, freshly ground white pepper
pinch of ground allspice
½ egg white
½ cup heavy cream, slightly frozen
1 teaspoon chopped fresh herbs: parsley, chive, marjoram
1 cup light chicken stock (see pages 52–3)

Dice the duck meat and the liver separately, season with salt, pepper, and allspice, cover with foil, and chill thoroughly in the refrigerator. In a food processor, first finely chop the diced duck meat, then add the liver and the egg white, and blend. Gradually mix in the cream. Push the forcemeat through a fine strainer and mix in the herbs. Using a teaspoon, form the forcemeat into fine gnocchi and poach in simmering stock for 2–3 minutes.

To make the squab filling: First roughly chop the squab breast and then chop it finely with a chopper. Press all the water out of the blanched spinach and chop the spinach finely.

RAVIOLI WITH SQUAB FILLING

These pasta pouches filled with poultry meat are very suitable as a garnish, particularly if the consommé is made from the same type of poultry. This squab meat filling is a real delicacy, but the ravioli can also be made with duck, guinea fowl, or quail.

Soak the toasted bread in milk, then squeeze dry and mix into the spinach.

Serves 8 as a soup garnish
For the pasta:
1¾ cups all-purpose flour, 2 eggs, 1 tablespoon olive oil, salt
For the filling:
6 oz skinless squab breast
1½ cups fresh spinach, blanched
1 slice toasted bread, milk for soaking
¼ cup each diced shallot and chopped mushroom
1 tablespoon olive oil
1 teaspoon each chopped fresh parsley and marjoram
salt, freshly ground white pepper
¼ cup heavy cream

Gently sweat the diced shallots and mushrooms in oil. Add the meat and sear.

Add the spinach mixture and the herbs and seasoning. Add the cream, and cook for 5 minutes over a medium heat.

Use the pasta ingredients to make a smooth dough. Allow it to rest, roll out thinly, and cut into small squares, or, as shown in the picture, into rounds. Make the filling as shown in the picture sequence to the right and distribute it on the pasta. Brush the edges of the pasta with water, fold over the filling, and press together. Poach in simmering salted water for 10–12 minutes.

These ravioli are suitable as a soup garnish, but can also be served as an appetizer or main course. They are delicious served with a paprika or tomato sauce and a generous topping of grated cheese.

CREAM OF POULTRY SOUP

The versatility of chicken stock is evident once again in this recipe, which allows a great deal of scope for your own creativity. You can vary it by using a different broth, additional seasoning ingredients, or different garnishes. Tender vegetables or poultry quenelles (see pages 56–7) go well with this soup. So, too, do strong spices, but be careful not to overpower the characteristic delicate taste of the chicken stock.

Serves 3
3 tablespoons unsalted butter
½ cup finely chopped leek
½ cup finely chopped celery
1 tablespoon all-purpose flour
5½ cups chicken broth (see pages 52–3)
1 lb finely chopped chicken bones
½ cup light cream
salt, freshly ground white pepper
freshly grated nutmeg

Make the soup as described in the picture sequence, and serve with the accompaniment of your choice.

Melt half the butter and lightly brown the finely chopped vegetables in it. Dust with flour and cook briefly before adding the chicken broth.

Cover the chicken bones with water and boil briefly. Drain, add to the broth and simmer for about 30 minutes. Add the cream and simmer for a further 5–10 minutes. Season the soup, pour through a conical strainer, and whisk in the remaining butter. Reheat before serving.

Cream soups
Use a lot of cream and a little flour

As a result of the amount of cream used, cream of poultry soups are not exactly low in calories, but they are nevertheless a light dish. The basic recipe can be varied easily. For example, heavy cream can be used instead of light cream, and a plain cream soup can be thickened with flour, as a result of which it becomes a *velouté*, with a wonderfully velvety consistency. The recipes here show that you can use only a minimal amount of flour and still achieve the desired smoothness. As an alternative, you can thicken cream soups with egg yolk, although this also makes them somewhat richer.

| 5 peppercorns |
| 2 whole allspice |
| 2 garlic cloves, lightly crushed |
| ½ cup light cream |
| salt |
| 4 heaping tablespoons finely chopped mixed fresh herbs, such as parsley, basil, sorrel, chervil, and chives |

Melt 2½ tablespoons of the butter in a large saucepan and sweat the shallots until they become transparent. Add the vegetables and cook until soft. Dust with flour and sweat again. Add the chicken broth and bring to a boil. Add the bay leaf, peppercorns, allspice, and garlic, and simmer gently over a low heat for approximately 30 minutes, skimming off any foam that rises to the surface. Add the cream, bring back to a boil, strain, and add salt. Add the herbs to the soup. Leave to infuse for a few minutes. Mix in the remaining butter, reheat, and serve. Suitable garnishes are finely diced chicken, quenelles, or croutons.

CREAM OF TURKEY SOUP WITH CUCUMBERS

Serves 3
1 lb chopped turkey bones
1 tablespoon vegetable oil
¼ cup diced onion
½ cup finely chopped celery
½ cup finely chopped carrot
½ cup diced cucumber
1½ tablespoons unsalted butter
1 tablespoon all-purpose flour
4½ cups poultry broth, preferably made from turkey (see pages 52–3)
5 peppercorns, 2 sprigs fresh parsley
½ cup light cream
For the garnish:
½ cup diced cucumber
1½ tablespoons unsalted butter
5 oz boiled or roast turkey breast
4 sprigs fresh dill

Chopped dill is the ideal way to complement the fresh flavor of the cucumbers.

Fry the turkey bones in the hot oil until golden brown, remove, and drain. In a large saucepan, cook the vegetables in the butter until soft. Dust with flour and brown lightly. Add the poultry broth, peppercorns, parsley, and the seared bones, and simmer for 30 minutes. Add the cream, stir, and bring to a boil. Pour through a fine conical strainer. To make the garnish, cook the diced cucumber in the butter until soft. Dice the turkey breast, and add to the soup with the cucumber. Reheat the soup and serve garnished with sprigs of dill.

CREAM OF HERBS SOUP

This is a robust cream soup, which still retains the characteristic flavor of the poultry.

Serves 3
¼ cup unsalted butter
⅓ cup diced shallot
¼ cup diced carrot
½ cup finely chopped leek
½ cup finely chopped celery
¼ cup finely chopped celeriac
1 tablespoon all-purpose flour
5½ cups chicken broth (see pages 52–3)
1 bay leaf

CREAM OF SQUAB SOUP

This cream soup is thickened with a little white bread and a lot of cream, and contains a crayfish to provide a counterpoint of flavor.

Serves 4

2 squabs
7 teaspoons unsalted butter
salt, freshly ground white pepper
1½ cups chopped leek
1 cup chopped carrots
1 cup chopped parsnips
1 cup chopped celery
1 garlic clove
1 sprig fresh thyme
6 cups light chicken stock (see pages 52–3)
4 crayfish
1 slice white bread without crusts
1¼ cups light cream
pinch of ground ginger
pinch of nutmeg
½ cup fresh sorrel

Wash the squabs inside and out, cut in half lengthwise with a pair of poultry shears, and dry. Heat the butter in a large saucepan until it foams, add the squabs, and brown lightly. Turn and cook the other side, and season with salt and pepper. Scatter the leeks, carrots, parsnips, and celery over the browned squabs. Use a heavy knife to crush the garlic clove without skinning it, and add it to the pot with the fresh thyme. Cover and braise for approximately 15 minutes. Add 1 cup of the chicken stock, cover the pot again, and continue to cook over a low heat for 40–50 minutes. Add the remaining stock, bring to a boil and simmer, uncovered, for 30 minutes over a very low heat.

Remove the squabs from the broth and keep warm. Strain the broth, pressing out the vegetables with a ladle. Wash the crayfish, twist off the tails by hand, and pull out the stomach and intestine. Bring the soup back to a boil. Soak the white bread in the cream, mix well, whisk into the soup, and simmer over a low heat for several minutes. Season with ginger and nutmeg. Cut the sorrel into strips, chop the squab meat, and add both to the soup. Leave to infuse with the crayfish for 10 minutes.

Cream of poultry soups

Substantial soups, thickly puréed with plenty of garnishes

All kinds of poultry can be used for these soups: lean chicken, squab, or even turkey, which works particularly well. They all combine superbly with vegetables, especially with celery and celeriac.

FRENCH CREAM OF CHICKEN SOUP

Serves 4
13 oz boneless chicken breasts
3¼ cups light chicken stock (see pages 52–3)
¼ cup unsalted butter
1 tablespoon all-purpose flour, 2¼ cups milk
10 oz mushrooms
2 teaspoons lemon juice
1 bunch fresh parsley
4 teaspoons Calvados
1 teaspoon salt
freshly ground white pepper
freshly grated nutmeg
1 cup light cream
2 egg yolks

Cook the chicken breasts in the stock over a low heat for approximately 15 minutes. Remove, and reserve the stock. Finely dice the meat and reserve. Heat half of the butter in a saucepan, add the flour and cook for 1–2 minutes. Whisk in half of the milk, cook gently for approximately 15 minutes, and reserve the completed béchamel sauce. Purée the washed mushrooms in the food processor and continue making the soup as shown in the picture sequence.

Place the purée in a bowl. Bring the remaining milk to a boil, pour over the purée and mix evenly.

Pour this mixture through a fine-mesh sieve into a suitably sized pot, add the stock, mix, and bring to a boil.

Add the mushroom sauce and mix in evenly with a whisk, season with salt, pepper, and nutmeg, and heat through again.

In a separate saucepan, reduce the cream by half, allow to cool slightly, then stir in the egg yolk. Pour this mixture into the soup to thicken it. Heat without boiling.

To make the cream of chicken soup:

Heat the remaining butter with the lemon juice and the parsley. Add the mushroom purée, and heat while stirring.

Add the béchamel sauce and bring to a boil, stirring vigorously with a whisk. Remove the parsley and reserve.

Put the chicken in a food processor, pour the Calvados on top, and purée into a fine, smooth paste.

Skinning peppers:
Roast the peppers in the
oven at 425°F until the
skins blister and dark
spots appear. Let cool,
then remove the skins.

To make the soup:

Heat the butter, add the sugar
and onions, and sweat. Add
the lemon juice and strips of
pepper, and stew for
approximately 5 minutes.

Add the chicken broth, bring to
the boil and simmer for
approximately 10 minutes. Add
the cream and simmer for a
further 10 minutes.

Halfway through the cooking
time add the garlic, thyme,
parsley, and rosemary, and
season with salt, pepper,
and ginger.

Remove the herbs and the
garlic, purée the soup in a
mixer, and strain. Add the
chicken meat and heat
through.

**With two different colored pepper
soups,** for example red and yellow,
interesting visual effects can be created.

CREAM OF CHICKEN SOUP WITH PEPPERS

In this recipe, plain chicken broth is turned into a
wholly new taste experience with cream and
peppers. The colors of the peppers also provide a
visual variation. You can use other vegetables — for
example, carrots, celery, or celeriac — to make
interesting taste combinations.

Serves 4

4 red or yellow peppers
7 teaspoons unsalted butter, 1 teaspoon sugar
¼ cup diced onion
2 tablespoons lemon juice
2¼ cups chicken broth (see pages 52–3)
½ cup light cream
1 garlic clove, lightly crushed
1 sprig each fresh thyme and parsley
fresh rosemary leaves
1 teaspoon salt
freshly ground white pepper
freshly grated ginger, to taste
2 poached chicken breasts, cut into strips

Skin the peppers, remove the pith and seeds, and
cut the flesh into strips. Make the soup as
described in the picture sequence to
the left. Then add the poached
chicken breast and heat
through slowly.

COCK-A-LEEKIE

This chicken soup originated in Scotland. As in the case of most traditional recipes, there are many different versions in circulation, but the basic ingredients are always the same, namely a boiling fowl, fresh leeks, and prunes. In some recipes, separately cooked pearl barley is added, making the soup somewhat more substantial.

Serves 4

one 4½-lb boiling fowl
9 cups water
2 teaspoons salt
1 small onion
1 sprig fresh parsley
1 sprig fresh thyme
1 blade mace
½ teaspoon black peppercorns
2 whole allspice
1 bay leaf
1½ lb leek
freshly ground white pepper and allspice
12 pitted prunes

Carefully wash the chicken inside and out and pat dry with paper towels. Pour the water into a large pot, add the chicken and the salt. Peel the onion, cut it in half, add it to the pot, and bring to a boil.

Add the parsley and the thyme. Tie the mace, peppercorns, and whole allspice in a small linen bag and add to the pot. Cut off the upper green leaves from the leeks and discard. Halve the leeks lengthwise, wash carefully, and cut into pieces about 2 inches long; add a quarter of them to the soup. Skim the foam from the surface and continue to cook slowly over a medium heat for 1½ hours.

Remove the tender cooked chicken, skin it, take the meat off the bones and cut it into pieces. Strain the broth, add the rest of the leek, and bring back to a boil. Reduce the heat and simmer until the leek is cooked. If necessary, adjust the seasoning with ground pepper and allspice. Add the chicken and the prunes. Remove the pot from the heat and leave to infuse for approximately 15 minutes.

To make the Sauce Supreme: Sweat the diced shallots in the butter, sprinkle with flour and cook briefly. Add the cold stock, mix evenly, and bring to a full boil. Add the cream, reduce, and strain.

SAUCE SUPRÊME

This is the finest of all poultry cream sauces and is frequently the basis of culinary delicacies.

Serves 4–6

1 shallot
1½ teaspoons unsalted butter
1 tablespoon all-purpose flour
2¼ cups light poultry stock (see pages 52–3)
½ cup heavy cream
pinch each of salt and cayenne pepper
dash of lemon juice

Peel the shallot and chop finely. Melt the butter in a pot, add the chopped shallot, and sweat until it becomes transparent. Sprinkle with flour and cook without allowing it to color. Add the cold poultry stock, stirring constantly, and mix until smooth. Simmer for 10 minutes, add the cream, and boil until the sauce has a creamy consistency. Season with salt, cayenne pepper, and lemon juice, and strain before serving.

WILD GARLIC SAUCE

Wild garlic, which is closely related to garlic, gives this sauce an interesting character. The leaves, which are mostly found in damp deciduous forests, are picked in May before they begin to blossom.

Not illustrated; serves 4

1 recipe Sauce Suprême
10 wild garlic leaves, 2 tablespoons whipped cream

Wash the wild garlic leaves, separate from the stalks, and chop finely. If desired, the stalks can be used in the base for the Sauce Suprême. Strain the sauce, add the chopped wild garlic leaves, and bring to a boil. Stir in the cream and serve.

MOREL SAUCE

Morels combine very well with poultry, and both dried and fresh morels can be used in this sauce.

Not illustrated; serves 4

¼ lb morels
1 recipe Sauce Velouté
1 shallot, 2 teaspoons unsalted butter
salt, freshly ground white pepper

If using dried morels, soak them first. Clean and wash the morels, and pat dry with paper towels. The scraps left after cleaning can be sweated with the shallot in the base for the Sauce Velouté, if desired. Strain the completed velouté and reserve. Peel and finely chop the shallot, and sweat in the hot butter until transparent. Add the morels, season with salt and pepper, mix, and cook for about 5 minutes. Add to the Sauce Velouté, heat through, and serve.

White poultry cream sauces
Versatile basic sauces thickened with flour

These white poultry cream sauces are served mainly with boiled or stewed light poultry meat, particularly turkey, boiling fowl, and young chickens. However, they can also be added to egg dishes or, for example, a dish of veal sweetbreads. You can vary these basic recipes by adding different herbs, mushrooms, and vegetables.

SAUCE VELOUTÉ

This simple poultry-based sauce can be refined at the end with a little whipped cream.

Serves 4–6

1 shallot
7 teaspoons unsalted butter
4 teaspoons all-purpose flour
½ cup white wine
3¼ cups light poultry stock (see pages 52–3)
pinch of salt
freshly ground white pepper
2 tablespoons whipped cream

Peel the shallot and dice finely. Melt the butter and sweat the shallot. Complete the velouté as described in the picture sequence below.

To make the Velouté:

Sprinkle the transparent shallots with the flour and cook a little, stirring constantly. Add the wine and mix evenly.

Add the cold chicken stock, mixing well with a whisk, and simmer gently for 12–15 minutes.

Season the sauce with salt and pepper, and strain. Just before serving, whisk in the whipped cream, but do not cook any longer.

CURRY SAUCE

For light sauces, you do not necessarily have to thicken poultry stock with a roux; you can achieve an equally good result with a *beurre manié*, equal quantities of butter and flour kneaded together. You can also add herbs and spices to the butter if desired. In this recipe, for example, curry is used. It is important that you cook the *beurre manié* long enough so that the sauce will not taste floury.

Serves 4–6

For the curry butter:
7 teaspoons unsalted butter, cubed
2½ teaspoons all-purpose flour
1 teaspoon curry powder
For the sauce:
2¼ cups light poultry stock (see pages 52–3)
½ cup light cream
pinch of salt
dash of lemon juice

Make the curry butter as described in the picture sequence to the right. Add it to the hot poultry stock, mix until thick and smooth, then simmer gently for about 15 minutes. Add the cream and reduce the sauce to a creamy consistency.

Steamed breast of chicken with green asparagus and cream of poultry sauce made with strips of fresh wild garlic.

Curry butter: Place the butter cubes on a plate with the flour and the curry powder, and knead with a fork. Shape into a roll and chill. To use, cut into small cubes.

Bring the poultry stock to the boil, add the cold butter cubes, and mix until smooth.

Add the cream and simmer gently for a further 5 minutes. Season with salt and lemon.

Piquant sauces for poultry

Strong, dark meat, like that of squab, duck, or goose, requires equally strong sauces, which support the characteristic taste. Such sauces are served mostly with poultry that has been quickly pan-fried or roasted whole. They can be combined with vegetables and herbs, fruits or spirits.

ROAST SQUAB WITH BLOOD ORANGE SAUCE

Blood oranges give the sauce a unique character and an intensive dark color.

Serves 2–4
For the sauce:
1½–1¾ lb blood oranges
1½ teaspoons chopped fresh ginger
1 cup dark poultry stock (see pages 50–1)
½ teaspoon cornstarch mixed with 3 tablespoons red wine
pinch of salt, freshly ground black pepper
Also:
two 11-oz squabs
salt, freshly ground white pepper
3 tablespoons vegetable oil

Make the sauce as shown below. Preheat the oven to 400°F. Wash the squabs inside and out, pat dry, season with salt and pepper, and truss with kitchen string. Heat the oil in a pan, quickly brown the squabs on the breast side, turn, and cook in the oven for 20–25 minutes. Remove, allow to rest briefly, remove the kitchen string, and serve the birds with the blood orange sauce.

Blood orange sauce: Extract the juice from two-thirds of the oranges. Reduce to a syrup with a little orange peel and the ginger. Add the stock, and reduce slightly. Add the cornstarch mixed with wine, and cook until thick. Add the remaining orange segments to the sauce, warm through (do not boil), and season.

ROAST DUCK BREAST WITH LENTIL SAUCE

The classic process of thickening poultry sauces with lentil purée is now only seldom seen, but it has earned its place in *haute cuisine*.

Serves 4
For the sauce:
¼ cup each green and red lentils
2¼ cups dark poultry stock (see pages 50–1)
1½ tablespoons cold unsalted butter cubes
salt, freshly ground white pepper
1 dash balsamic vinegar
1 tablespoon finely chopped fresh chives
Also:
4 duck breasts, 7 oz each
salt
freshly ground white pepper
¼ cup vegetable oil

Wash the different types of lentils separately and cook in salted water. Drain the red lentils after approximately 8 minutes and rinse with cold water. Cook the green lentils for 18–23 minutes and drain when soft. While still warm, purée the green lentils with a hand-held mixer, strain, and reserve. Make the sauce as described in the picture sequence below left.

Preheat the oven to 350–400°F. Season the duck breasts with salt and pepper. Heat the oil in a pan, brown the breasts on the skin side and roast in the oven. Turn only when the skin is crispy. After 10–12 minutes, remove, allow to rest briefly, and cut into equal slices. Garnish with the lentil sauce and serve.

MADEIRA SAUCE

Not illustrated; serves 4

½ cup Madeira

1 cup dark poultry stock (see pages 50–1)

2 teaspoons cold unsalted butter

salt, freshly ground white pepper

Pour the Madeira into a saucepan and reduce until little remains. Add the poultry stock and reduce to approximately half over a low heat. Thicken with the cold butter and season.

RED ONION SAUCE

For this easy-to-make sauce, which is ideal with strong poultry meat, no poultry stock is required. The red onions give the sauce its wonderful color.

Serves 4

¾ lb red onions

2 teaspoons unsalted butter

1 sprig fresh thyme

½ cup port

2¼ cups red wine

2½ tablespoons cold unsalted butter, cubed

salt, freshly ground white pepper

Lentil sauce: Bring the poultry stock to a boil, add the green lentil purée and mix in well. Mix in the red lentils. Whisk the cold butter cubes into the sauce, season with salt, pepper, and balsamic vinegar, sprinkle with the chives, and serve with the freshly roasted duck breast.

Red onion sauce: Peel the onions and chop finely. Heat the butter in a saucepan and sweat the onions. Add the sprig of thyme. Pour in the port, reduce to half, then add the red wine and simmer for 25–30 minutes. Whisk the cold butter cubes into the sauce. Season with salt and pepper.

Poaching and steaming

The three moist cooking methods — boiling, poaching, and steaming — are, admittedly, not the main ones used for cooking poultry, but they are nonetheless irreplaceable. Boiling is generally used only for the preparation of stocks and broths (see pages 48–67), where a strong concentration is required. When tender, young poultry meat is to be eaten, the   gentler cooking methods of poaching and steaming are more appropriate.

In poaching, the meat cooks slowly in liquid at the hottest possible temperature below boiling point, generally between 167°F and 194°F. It is important to start with cold liquid and to bring it just to the boiling point so that the scum rises to the surface and can be skimmed off. The amount and quality of the liquid also affect the taste of the meat, as during cooking a continual exchange takes place between them. When poaching poultry in water, the pot should be large enough for the bird to be completely covered by the liquid, but no larger, in order to keep the amount of liquid to a minimum. When the meat is poached in a stock, the volume of liquid can be higher, and therefore the pot can be larger if necessary.

In steaming, the meat is cooked in a perforated container over boiling water in a covered pot. This is a particularly gentle method. Steaming causes the least loss of nutrients and preserves the maximum characteristic taste.

Poaching and steaming poultry are the best ways to capture the characteristic taste of the meat.
This strength of flavor will also be evident in the sauce,
which should be very modestly seasoned.

1 Pull out the neck glands and the fat on the skin of the neck, and cut off carefully.

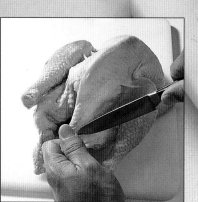

2 Cut two small slits in the skin on the left and right side of the abdominal opening.

3 Push the drumsticks through the slits in the skin so that they do not point upward.

4 Place the chicken in a saucepan. Surround it with the vegetables, cut into large pieces.

5 Add sufficient cold water to cover the chicken completely, and bring just to a boil.

6 Carefully skim off the foam, then reduce the heat so that the liquid shimmers but does not bubble.

7 Add a large sprig of parsley, 1 bay leaf, and 1 teaspoon of black peppercorns to the chicken.

8 Poach the chicken for 1–1½ hours. Remove it from the stock, allow it to cool, and then cut it into pieces.

Poaching a chicken
Cooking just below boiling point

Poaching is particularly suitable for boiling fowl, whose meat, while not as tender as that of a younger bird, still becomes soft, and the gelatin in it makes the resultant broth extremely tasty. Controlling the temperature is the real art of poaching, for the liquid must be kept boiling hot but must not actually boil!

To poach a chicken, place it in a saucepan large enough for it to remain covered with liquid throughout its cooking time. Cover it with cold water or stock; water becomes rich in flavor and can be served as a light soup; stock serves as the basis for the sauce. Bring the liquid slowly to just below the boiling point. Skim off the foam that forms, and adjust the heat so that the broth barely bubbles.

When poaching poultry, it is usual to cook vegetables with it. The recipe on this page uses 2 small carrots, 1 onion, 1 leek, and 1 celeriac.

A firm corn-fed chicken: The color of the meat depends on the type of feed the chicken consumed during its life. This chicken was fed predominantly on corn.

1 After separating the legs from the carcass, pull off the skin; it will come off quite easily.

To cut up a cooked boiling fowl: The number of pieces obtained may vary according to the size of the bird. In this picture sequence, the boiling fowl is cut up with the skin on.

1 Lay the chicken on its back, and make an incision in the skin between the leg and the breast.

2 Completely remove the skin from the breast meat while it is still on the carcass.

2 Locate where the leg bone joins the body. Cut through the joint and splay apart. Remove the leg.

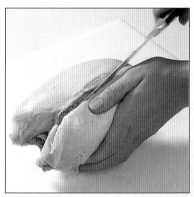

3 Carefully remove the breasts from the carcass, slicing down on either side of the backbone.

4 The meat of the individual pieces, with the skin on or removed, can be used as a garnish for soup and for fricassees or salads.

3 Turn the carcass 180°, cut along the breast bone and remove the breast. Cut off the wings.

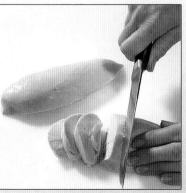

4 Cut up the tender breast meat as directed in recipes for terrines, aspic, or salads.

To make a *pot-au-feu*:

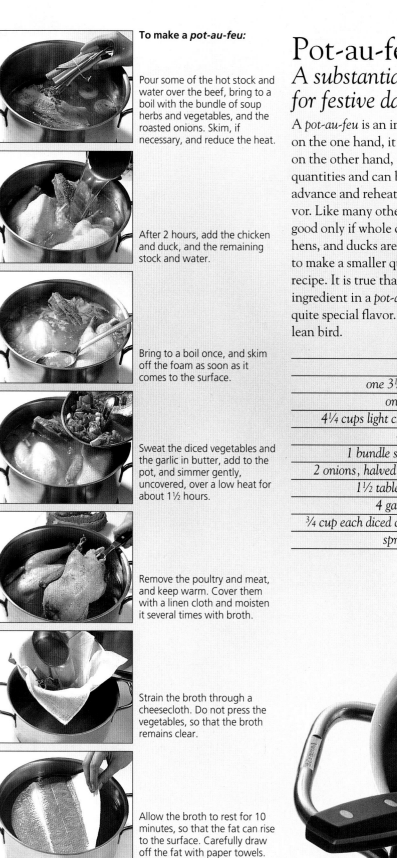

Pour some of the hot stock and water over the beef, bring to a boil with the bundle of soup herbs and vegetables, and the roasted onions. Skim, if necessary, and reduce the heat.

After 2 hours, add the chicken and duck, and the remaining stock and water.

Bring to a boil once, and skim off the foam as soon as it comes to the surface.

Sweat the diced vegetables and the garlic in butter, add to the pot, and simmer gently, uncovered, over a low heat for about 1½ hours.

Remove the poultry and meat, and keep warm. Cover them with a linen cloth and moisten it several times with broth.

Strain the broth through a cheesecloth. Do not press the vegetables, so that the broth remains clear.

Allow the broth to rest for 10 minutes, so that the fat can rise to the surface. Carefully draw off the fat with paper towels.

Place the poultry and the beef in another pot and pour the broth over them. Cut the vegetables into large pieces, add to the pot, and cook gently for 10 minutes. Finally, add the cooked beans, season with salt and pepper, and reheat.

Pot-au-feu of poultry
A *substantial meal* for festive days

A *pot-au-feu* is an inherently festive meal because, on the one hand, it is a highly decorative dish and, on the other hand, it is ideal for making in large quantities and can be prepared several days in advance and reheated later without any loss of flavor. Like many other dishes, *pot-au-feu* tastes really good only if whole chickens, particularly roasting hens, and ducks are cooked quite slowly. If you want to make a smaller quantity, halve the following recipe. It is true that duck is a somewhat unusual ingredient in a *pot-au-feu*, but it does contribute a quite special flavor. It is important to use a young, lean bird.

Serves 6–8
1¾ lb brisket
one 3½-lb roasting chicken
one 1¾-lb duckling
4¼ cups light chicken stock (see pages 52–3)
4¼ cups water
1 bundle soup herbs and vegetables
2 onions, halved and roasted until golden brown
1½ tablespoons unsalted butter
4 garlic cloves, crushed
¾ cup each diced celery, carrot, onion, and tomato
sprigs of fresh thyme

The *pot-au-feu* can be transformed into the Italian dish, *bollito misto* with a stuffed leg of pork, an addition that complements the poultry well. The dish then also needs a *salsa verde*, the typical Italian green sauce.

For the vegetable garnish:

³⁄₄ *cup navy beans, soaked overnight*

1–2 leeks, 2 celery stalks, 3 zucchini

To accompany:

boiled potatoes

salt, pepper, 1 tablespoon chopped fresh parsley

Wash the beef and poultry, and pat dry with paper towels. Remove the abdominal fat from the chicken and the duck. Continue as described in the picture sequence on the opposite page.

Cook the navy beans in fresh water with the leeks, celery, and zucchini for up to 1 hour, until soft.

To serve, remove the fat from the beef, and slice the meat. Divide the chicken into portions. Remove the skin from the duck and divide the bird into portions. Arrange the meats in soup plates with boiled potatoes, pour the broth on top, season with salt and pepper, and sprinkle with parsley. If you want to enrich the *pot-au-feu* with sausage or a stuffed leg of pork, add it to the pot 10 minutes before serving and heat it through.

Poultry in fine broth

These "one-pot meals" are light, but strong in taste. Poached poultry dishes are light, as the recipes on these two pages demonstrate, because they contain so little fat. Both dishes get their particularly strong taste from being poached in poultry stock instead of water. The vegetables impart an appetizing aroma and additional flavor.

POULE AU POT

This "hen in the pot" is a substantial, complete meal. It can be enjoyed as a combined dish, like a stew, or you can serve the broth separately as an appetizer, and the meat and vegetables as the main course.

Serves 4

one 4-lb roasting chicken, with heart and gizzard
¾ cup chopped carrots
¾ cup chopped celery
¾ cup baby white turnips
¼ cup celeriac
2 cups chopped Savoy cabbage
4¼ cups light chicken stock (see pages 52–3)
1 onion, studded with 2 cloves
20 peppercorns
1 teaspoon salt

Wash the chicken inside and out, pat dry carefully, and fix the drumsticks as shown on pages 70–1. Place in a suitably sized pot and cover with water. Bring to a boil once over a high heat to blanch. Pour off the water, rinse the chicken with cold water and return to the pot with the gizzard and heart. Add the chopped vegetables to the pot and fill with the chicken stock. Bring to a boil, then reduce the heat so that the liquid remains just below boiling point. From time to time, skim off any scum or foam that comes to the surface. Add the onion, peppercorns, and salt, and continue to poach the chicken for 50–60 minutes, until tender. Cut the chicken into portions and serve.

SQUABS IN THE POT

Poached squab has an extremely delicate taste, particularly when accompanied by the right vegetables and swimming in a suitably concentrated broth. In this way squabs can be served as a first course, or, accompanied, for example, by potatoes, they can provide a substantial main course.

Serves 4 as a first course

two ½-lb squabs
For the lentils:
½ cup red lentils
5 tablespoons diced onion
¼ cup peanut oil
1 cup water
1 garlic clove, lightly crushed
¾ cup chopped celery
¾ cup chopped leek
½ cup chopped carrots
¾ cup chopped baby white turnips
3 ¼ cups light poultry stock (see pages 52–3)
1 teaspoon salt
freshly ground white pepper
1 bay leaf
1 sprig fresh thyme
1 bunch fresh flat-leaf parsley

Wash the squabs inside and out and dry carefully. Place them in a saucepan, cover with water, bring to a boil to blanch, and immediately pour off the water. Rinse the squabs with cold water.

Wash the lentils thoroughly. Briefly fry 2 tablespoons of diced onions in 1 tablespoon hot oil, add the lentils, pour on the water, and cook until almost soft. Heat the remaining oil in another saucepan, fry the remaining diced onion and add the garlic. Add the chopped vegetables and cook, stirring constantly, until they are lightly colored. Place the squabs on top, pour on the stock, bring to a boil, and immediately reduce the heat. Do not cover the pot, and be sure to keep the liquid below boiling for the remainder of the cooking time. After about 20 minutes, add salt, pepper, bay leaf, thyme, parsley, and the lentils, and continue to poach, until the squabs and the vegetables are tender.

Place the stuffing in the middle of the boned chicken. Fold the bird back together. Push into shape, sew up with string, and truss as described on page 26.

STUFFED CHICKEN WITH RED ONION SAUCE

Serves 4

one 2-lb chicken

6¼ cups light chicken stock (see pages 52–3)

1 bouquet garni

For the stuffing:

5 oz veal, well chilled

¾ cup diced carrots

½ cup diced zucchini

¾ cup heavy cream

7 oz mushrooms, finely diced

salt, freshly ground white pepper

For the onion sauce:

2 teaspoons unsalted butter

3½ cups diced red onions

1 sprig fresh thyme

½ cup port

2¼ cups red wine

2½ tablespoons cold unsalted butter

salt, freshly ground white pepper

Wash the chicken thoroughly inside and out, and pat dry. Bone the chicken from the back, but leave the wing and leg bones intact (see page 41). To make the stuffing, purée the veal in a food processor, then chill. Press the purée through a fine strainer and chill again. Blanch the carrots and zucchini and drain well. Whip 1 tablespoon of the cream until stiff. Thoroughly mix the veal with the remaining cream and the carrots, zucchini, and mushrooms. Season with salt and pepper, and fold in the whipped cream. Stuff the chicken as shown in the picture sequence to the left. Bring the stock to a boil. Place the stuffed chicken and the bouquet garni in the stock, and poach for 1½ hours, partially covered.

To make the onion sauce, heat the butter in a saucepan and sweat the onions. Add the thyme. Pour in the port, reduce to half, add the red wine, and simmer for 25–30 minutes. Cut the cold butter into cubes and add a few at a time, stirring constantly, then whisk into the sauce. Season.

CHICKEN STUFFED WITH TRUFFLES

In French cuisine this extravagant and sumptuous dish is known as *poulet demi-deuil*, or "half-mourning chicken." The strong aroma of the black truffles dominates this delicacy.

Serves 4

one 4-lb roasting chicken
1 fresh truffle, approximately ¾ oz
For the stuffing:
1½ tablespoons unsalted butter, 1 cup chicken liver
2 slices white bread without crusts, 4 tablespoons milk
1 egg, 4 teaspoons brandy
⅓ teaspoon salt, ⅓ teaspoon freshly ground white pepper
For cooking:
1 carrot
1 small, halved onion, 2 celery stalks
1 bouquet garni, 10 peppercorns
9 cups light poultry stock (see pages 52–3)
1 cup dry white wine
For the sauce:
7 teaspoons unsalted butter, 1 tablespoon flour,
1 egg yolk, ½ cup light cream

Wash the chicken thoroughly inside and out, drain, and pat dry. Brush the truffle well under cold running water and cut into thin slices. To make the stuffing, heat the butter, brown the livers on all sides, remove, and dice finely. Soak the bread in the milk, squeeze out, and place in a bowl with the liver, egg, brandy, salt, and pepper, and mix well. Mix in any scraps left after cleaning the truffle. Stuff the chicken as shown in the picture sequence to the right.

Put the vegetables with the bouquet garni and the peppercorns into the stock, add the white wine, heat, and simmer for 15 minutes. Poach the stuffed chicken in the liquid until done, remove and keep warm. Strain the stock and reduce to approximately 2¼ cups. To make the sauce, melt the butter, add the flour and cook for 1–2 minutes. Pour on the reduced stock and stir to form a light sauce. Simmer for 15 minutes. Combine the egg yolk and the cream, and add to the sauce to thicken it. Add the chicken to the sauce and heat through.

To stuff the chicken: Loosen the skin from the neck. Work forward carefully with the fingers from the breast toward the legs.

Push the truffle slices between the skin and the flesh, and distribute as evenly as possible over the breast and legs.

Season the cavity with salt and pepper, then add the liver forcemeat with a spoon, taking care not to overfill.

Carefully sew up the opening, truss the chicken, and wrap it in a cotton kitchen towel.

Place the chicken in the prepared broth and slowly bring to a boil, uncovered. Poach for 1½ hours.

To make the blanquette:

Skin the turkey meat, cut into 1-inch cubes, and blanch in boiling salted water.

Allow the water to bubble briefly until all the sediment has risen to the surface, then drain the meat.

Thoroughly rinse the diced turkey in cold water to remove any residue that might remain.

Place the meat in the stock, bring to a boil, and add the bouquet garni, studded onion, bay leaf, and a pinch of salt.

Cook for 1 hour, then drain the meat and reserve the cooking liquid.

To make the roux, melt the butter in a saucepan and add the flour, stirring continuously.

Slowly add the white wine, stirring continuously until smooth.

Simmer gently for about 12 minutes. Then add the cream and reduce the sauce slightly.

Gradually add the reserved cooking liquid, mixing well with a whisk, and bring to a boil.

Season with salt, pepper and lemon. Heat the turkey pieces in the sauce and incorporate the egg sauce.

Blanquette
Serving the meat in plenty of sauce

The blanquette differs from the much better-known fricassee in that the meat is cooked first and the sauce is made separately afterward. The meat for the blanquette is, as a rule, also diced more finely, as for a ragout. Preparing the meat and sauce separately makes it possible to create new dishes by adding spices and other seasoning ingredients. The sauce can be varied, for example, with paprika or curry, as well as with precooked aromatic vegetables, turning the blanquette into a ragout.

BLANQUETTE OF TURKEY LEG

This basic recipe for a blanquette can be varied as desired. It can be made with all types of poultry, although turkey is particularly suitable, and it does not always have to be the finest meat from the breast.

Serves 4

1½ lb boneless turkey thigh
For the bouquet garni:
1 small carrot, ½ leek, 1 piece celeriac
1 sprig fresh parsley
½ onion studded with 2 cloves,
1 bay leaf
For the sauce:
6½ cups light poultry stock (see pages 52–3)
2 teaspoons unsalted butter, 1½ teaspoons flour
½ cup white wine, ½ cup light cream

salt, freshly ground white pepper
1 dash lemon juice
1 egg yolk
2 tablespoons heavy cream, lightly whipped

Skin and dice the turkey meat. Clean the vegetables for the bouquet garni, cut into pieces of equal size and tie with kitchen string. Stud the onion half with the cloves and the bay leaf. Make the blanquette as shown in the picture sequence to the left. Heat the meat through again in the sauce. Combine the egg yolk and cream and stir into the sauce. Do not cook the sauce any more.

This basic recipe can be refined as desired with various vegetables – such as asparagus, cauliflower, mushrooms, tiny braised onions – or even with fruit, as in both of the recipes below.

BLANQUETTE WITH MANGO AND SHRIMP

Serves 4

1 ripe mango
12 large cooked shrimp or prawns

Peel the mango, remove the pit, and cut the flesh into cubes. Add to the finished blanquette with the shrimp or prawns. Thicken and garnish as desired with fresh lemon balm.

Turkey Blanquette with mango and prawns (left), and with peas and tomatoes (below).

BLANQUETTE WITH TOMATOES AND PEAS

Serves 4

¾ lb tomatoes
½ cup peas

Blanch, peel, quarter, and seed the tomatoes. Cut the flesh into small wedges. Add the tomatoes and peas to the sauce before adding the egg and cream, and heat through with the meat.

Steaming poultry

A gentle cooking method for the finest cuts

Cooking in steam is probably the gentlest cooking method for tender pieces of poultry. For this, the meat is placed on a steamer tray, or even in a strainer or colander, and cooked over boiling water in a covered pot. The basic recipe can be enhanced by adding aromatic ingredients, but these should not be so strong that they mask the characteristic taste of the poultry.

SQUAB BREAST STEAMED IN BEET LEAVES

Serves 4

8 squab breasts, about 3 oz each

10–12 large beet leaves

1½ tablespoons soft unsalted butter

salt, freshly ground white pepper

For the sauce:

⅔ cup light poultry stock (see pages 52–3)

7 teaspoons each milk and light cream

1 slice white bread without crusts

2 tablespoons freshly grated horseradish or 1 tablespoon prepared horseradish

salt, freshly ground white pepper

a few dashes of lemon juice

1 tablespoon whipped cream

Remove the stalks from the beet leaves, wash the leaves and blanch them in boiling salted water. Refresh with cold water, remove the central ribs, and spread out to dry on a cloth. Skin the washed squab breasts, remove the sinews, and continue as described in the picture sequence.

To make the sauce, bring the stock to a boil with the milk and cream, reduce the heat and simmer for about 5 minutes. Dice the bread, add it to the liquid, and heat briefly. Remove the pot from the heat, add the horseradish, allow to infuse briefly, and strain the sauce. Before serving, reheat, but do not boil; season with salt, pepper, and lemon juice, and stir in the cream. Cut open the squab packages and arrange on the horseradish sauce.

To steam the beet leaf packages:
Lay out the beet leaves in rectangles and brush with the butter. Place a squab breast as shown, and season with salt and pepper. Fold the sides over the breast and wrap the breast completely.

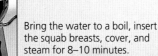

Put a small amount of water in a saucepan; it must not come into contact with the bottom of the steamer tray.

Bring the water to a boil, insert the squab breasts, cover, and steam for 8–10 minutes.

SQUAB STEAMED ON VEGETABLES

In this recipe the tender meat of the squabs benefits from the fresh flavor of the vegetables, and the sherry imparts a note of piquancy.

Not illustrated; serves 4

two 1-lb squabs

½ teaspoon salt

freshly ground white pepper

pinch of ground ginger

4 sprigs fresh tarragon

4¼ cups light poultry stock (see pages 52–3)

1 onion

2–3 celery stalks

2–3 small zucchini

1–2 baby white turnips

5 tablespoons unsalted butter

⅓ cup dry sherry

½ cup light cream

Wash the squabs thoroughly and pat dry inside and out. Season the cavity with salt, pepper, and ginger,

To complement the taste of steamed poultry, serve it with carrots, kohlrabi, celery, and potatoes.

STEAMED YOUNG GUINEA FOWL STUFFED WITH VEGETABLES AND HERBS

Steaming makes the guinea fowl easily digestible, while the aromatic foods steamed with it further enhance its characteristic taste.

Serves 2
two ¾-lb young guinea fowls
For the stuffing:
2 tablespoons chopped fresh parsley
1 teaspoon fresh lemon thyme
1½ tablespoons soft unsalted butter
salt, freshly ground white pepper
1 carrot
½ celeriac
1 celery stalk

Wash the guinea fowls inside and out under running water and carefully pat dry. To make the stuffing, chop the herbs, mix with the butter, and season with salt and pepper. Wash and peel the vegetables, and cut them into strips. Stuff the guinea fowls under the skin as described in the picture sequence, and steam for 25 minutes. To serve, halve or slice the guinea fowl, and serve with the vegetables if desired. A light sauce, a sabayon, or a salad is an ideal accompaniment for this dish.

and place 2 sprigs of tarragon in each. To fix the legs, make small slits in the flaps of skin either side of the stomach and push the legs through. Reduce the poultry stock to half. Peel and quarter the onion. Clean the vegetables and cut into pieces of equal size. Melt 1½ tablespoons of butter in a saucepan, and lightly sweat the onions and vegetables. Chill the remaining butter. Add the reduced stock and sherry to the saucepan, and place the prepared squabs on top. Steam, covered, for about 40 minutes, then take out the squabs, wrap in foil, and keep warm. Strain the cooking liquid, pressing the vegetables lightly, and reduce to approximately 1 cup. Whisk in the cream and boil down for a few minutes. Adjust the seasoning if necessary. Finally, beat in the cold butter with a hand-held mixer. Cut the squabs lengthwise, arrange on 4 plates, and spoon over the sauce. This dish goes well with truffled noodles or with steamed potatoes garnished with plenty of herbs.

To stuff and steam guinea fowl:

Using your fingers, carefully loosen the skin of the guinea fowl without damaging it, working from the neck along the breast.

Push the herb butter under the skin with the aid of a teaspoon and spread it evenly over the breasts.

Season the cavity with salt and pepper, and carefully insert the prepared vegetables.

Tie the stuffed guinea fowl into shape with kitchen string and steam in a covered pot.

Stewing and braising

Stewing and braising are both slow, moist-heat methods of cooking that are usually employed for relatively tough cuts of meat, including drumsticks, and for older poultry, for which they are ideal. They also provide a welcome alternative to the more common frying, roasting, and broiling used for the more tender cuts of poultry. In stewing, the poultry is not browned first, but is cooked slowly in a little liquid at a moderate temperature, so that the meat is scarcely colored. The meat then continues to stew in the liquid and the steam that is given off during cooking.

Braising is quite different. It always starts with vigorously browning the meat in a little fat, creating a roasted quality. Then the liquid is added and the heat reduced, so the browned crust softens in the moist heat, and the flavors of the meat and liquid are developed and exchanged. Braising uses less liquid than stewing and a slightly longer simmering time. It is particularly good for enhancing the flavors and increasing the tenderness of drumsticks and meat of older animals. In both methods, the taste of the poultry can be be varied by adding vegetables, spices, herbs, and wine.

Rustic regional braised chicken dishes,
such as this *pollo alla cacciatore*, are distinctive because
the vigorous browning gives them a lot of flavor.

STEWED BREAST OF GUINEA FOWL

The tiny guinea fowl provides us with some of the finest quality poultry meat, so stewing, which is a particularly gentle cooking method, is simply ideal. As the tender flesh cooks very quickly, the vegetables must be young and of the best quality. It is best to chop any large vegetables finely so that they cook at the same time as the meat.

Serves 2

4 breasts of guinea fowl, 3 oz each
2 teaspoons unsalted butter
salt
freshly ground white pepper
For the sauce:
¼ cup finely chopped shallots
½ cup finely chopped leek
⅓ cup finely chopped carrots
¼ cup finely chopped celeriac
½ cup light poultry stock (see pages 52–3)
½ cup light cream
1 teaspoon chopped fresh tarragon
dash of champagne vinegar

Scrape away the meat on the lower wings to expose the bones. Prepare the dish as shown in the picture sequence below. Serve the breasts in the sauce, accompanied by noodles, rice, or potatoes.

CHOPPED TURKEY BREAST

This recipe is a good example of how the larger cuts of poultry, such as the breast of roasting chickens and ducks or turkeys, can be simply and delicately stewed.

Serves 2

10 oz chopped turkey breast
salt
freshly ground white pepper
1 shallot
½ garlic clove
2 cooked artichoke hearts
½ lb tomatoes
2 tablespoons olive oil
1 teaspoon unsalted butter
¼ cup white wine
1 teaspoon fresh rosemary leaves
2 tablespoons crème fraîche (optional)

Cut the turkey into short strips approximately ½-inch thick, and season with salt and pepper. Peel and finely dice the shallot, and crush the garlic. Cut the artichoke hearts into wedges. Scald, skin, quarter, and seed the tomatoes. Make the dish as described in the picture sequence below. Add crème fraîche for a milder sauce. Serve with a risotto, polenta, or fine noodles.

Heat the butter until foaming. Season the breasts with salt and pepper, and brown lightly on the skin side. Add the shallots, leek, carrots, and celeriac, and sweat them. Pour in the poultry stock and reduce. Then add the cream and reduce again. Season the sauce with salt and pepper, add the tarragon, and then add the vinegar.

Heat the olive oil with the butter and sear the turkey meat without allowing it to color. Add the shallots, the garlic, and the wedges of artichoke, and sweat them. Add the white wine. Add the tomatoes and simmer for 6–8 minutes. When the liquid has evaporated and the tomatoes are soft, sprinkle the rosemary leaves on top, and adjust the seasoning before serving.

Pot-roasting

Another cooking method for fine cuts of poultry

Pot-roasting is an intermediate stage between stewing and braising that usually refers to cooking a single, large piece of meat or, in the case of poultry, a whole bird. Whereas in stewing, the meat is, at most, only lightly colored, and in braising it is definitely browned, in pot-roasting it is lightly browned before cooking in a lot of liquid. To give more color to a stewed or pot-roasted dish, it can be placed uncovered in the oven after the end of the cooking. The dry air in the oven causes the surface to brown, and frequent basting gives additional luster.

POT-ROASTED SQUABS IN SAUTERNES

The squabs are first cooked in plenty of butter, which helps them to develop a light color. The sweet, fruity and full-bodied Sauternes goes very well with the squabs, which must be basted several times during cooking.

Serves 2
two 11-oz squabs
salt
freshly ground white pepper
3 tablespoons unsalted butter
½ cup Sauternes
½ cup light poultry stock (see pages 52–3)
2 tablespoons crème fraîche
seedless grapes

Wash the squabs, pat dry, season the cavity of each with salt and pepper, and truss with kitchen string. Season the skin with salt and pepper, and prepare the squabs as described in the picture sequence to the right. The repeated basting with the butter sauce gives the squabs a shiny, glazed surface. Serve them with pasta, such as truffled noodles, and sauerkraut cooked with champagne.

After cooking the squabs season the sauce with salt and pepper, add the grapes, and heat through. Remove the kitchen string from the squabs, arrange them on a serving dish, and pour the sauce on top.

Squabs in Sauternes:

Heat the butter until foaming and quickly brown the prepared squabs on all sides.

Place the squabs on their backs, pour on the Sauternes, and reduce to half.

Add the poultry stock and simmer until cooked, basting the squabs several times with the sauce.

Remove the squabs and keep warm. Add the cold *crème fraîche* to the stock and mix in well.

There are many ways to vary this recipe. Instead of the lobster, you can use a crayfish of equal weight. It, too, should be precooked and cut, and the claws must be cracked with a heavy knife, so that the flavor of their meat can blend into the sauce. Or you might prefer to combine the lobster with squab. In this case, substitute two squabs for the chicken, and red wine for the champagne, and omit the brandy and saffron.

CHAMPAGNE CHICKEN WITH LOBSTER

Serves 4
one 2½-lb chicken with the liver
salt
freshly ground white pepper
pinch of cinnamon
one 1¼-lb lobster
4 tomatoes
1 small onion
¼ cup unsalted butter
1 bouquet garni, consisting of fresh marjoram, thyme, and parsley
1 bay leaf
½ cup champagne
4 teaspoons brandy
6 tablespoons vegetable oil
5 saffron threads
2 garlic cloves
2 tablespoons toasted almonds
1 teaspoon cornstarch (optional)

Rinse the chicken under cold running water and dry well inside and out with paper towels. Rub salt, pepper, and cinnamon well into the skin and divide into 8 pieces (see pages 24–5). Place the lobster in boiling water and cook for 5 minutes. Remove, drain well, and pat dry with paper towels. Using a strong serrated knife, cut the tail and body into 4 parts. Scald the tomatoes with boiling water, remove the skin, and finely dice the flesh. Finely chop the onion.

Heat the butter in a large saucepan, add the chicken pieces with the liver and fry, turning continuously, until golden brown. Add the onion, the tomatoes, the bouquet garni, and the bay leaf to the chicken and braise everything for 5–10 minutes. Remove the chicken liver from the pan. Add the champagne and brandy to the cooking liquid, boil to reduce by half, then add sufficient hot water to cover the chicken pieces. Braise over a low heat for approximately 10 minutes. Heat the oil in a clean pan, add the pieces of lobster, and brown quickly. As soon as the flesh begins to firm, add to the chicken pieces in their pot and braise for a further 10 minutes or until tender.

In a mortar, grind the saffron with the peeled garlic cloves, the almonds and the chicken liver, and mix well. Dilute this paste with a little water and stir into the pan. Season with salt and pepper. Reduce the sauce well, and strain if necessary. If you prefer a slightly thicker sauce, add the cornstarch mixed with a little water and boil to the desired consistency. Serve this dish with fresh white bread or rice and a light salad.

Chicken and lobster

A delicate combination for a festive meal

Chicken and lobster are a popular combination in many cuisines. In this recipe the delicate flavor of the chicken and the complementary richness of the lobster are accentuated by ripe tomatoes and fresh herbs. The taste of the dish is rounded off by the acidity of the champagne. This can, of course, be replaced with a dry, sparkling white wine, which should then also be served with the meal.

A simpler version can be made using unmarinated chicken pieces. Remove them from the pan after browning. Sweat the onions and the tomatoes in the spicy oil, then return the meat to the pan.

POLLO ALLA CACCIATORE

A chicken dish with this name is found in most Italian provinces, but each region has its own recipe. In all of them, however, the chicken is spiced with plenty of garlic, and black olives are an essential ingredient. It is the latter in particular that give this dish its unmistakable Mediterranean taste. Capers and anchovies are often also added.

Serves 4
one 4½-lb chicken
For the paste:
3 tablespoons fine olive oil
1 teaspoon salt, freshly ground white pepper
pinch fresh rosemary leaves
1 teaspoon fresh oregano
zest of ½ lemon
2 garlic cloves
Also:
2 tablespoons olive oil
⅓ cup diced onion
2 tomatoes
16 pitted black olives
2 anchovy fillets
2 teaspoons salted capers

Wash the chicken inside and out, and pat dry. Cut into 4 or 8 pieces. In a mortar, grind together all the ingredients for the paste, and coat the chicken pieces with it. Leave to marinate in a covered dish for 1–2 hours.

Heat the 2 tablespoons of oil in a frying pan, fry the marinated chicken pieces one after the other on all sides until crispy and brown, remove and keep warm. Add the diced onion to the spicy oil in the frying pan, and sweat them. Blanch the tomatoes, remove the skin, and dice the flesh. Add to the onions, cook for 2–3 minutes and return the chicken pieces to the pan. Cover and braise for approximately 20 minutes. Cut the olives into halves, if desired, and cut the anchovies into pieces. Add to the pan at the same time as the capers and braise for a further 10–15 minutes, until the meat is tender. Risotto is a classic accompaniment.

Robust regional fare

Braised poultry for simple, hearty meals

These recipes have evolved over the years. Based on regional products, they are uncomplicated and robust, and popular for precisely that reason.

GUINEA FOWL IN PAPRIKA SAUCE

This type of preparation for poultry is commonly found in the cuisines of Austria and Hungary.

Serves 4

two 1¼-lb guinea fowls
salt, freshly ground white pepper
1 yellow, 1 red pepper
2 tomatoes, 2 tablespoons vegetable oil, 7 teaspoons unsalted butter
1 garlic clove, 1¼ cups diced onion
5 teaspoons sweet paprika
½ cup dark poultry stock (see pages 50–1)
½ cup light cream, 1 teaspoon fresh marjoram

Wash the guinea fowls inside and out, and pat dry. Split them lengthwise, and season with salt and pepper. Roast the peppers in the oven at 425°F until the skin blisters and browns. Allow to cool slightly, remove the skin, seeds, and pith, and cut the flesh into strips. Blanch, skin, and seed the tomatoes, and cut the flesh into quarters. Continue as described in the picture sequence to the right. Then return the halves of guinea fowl to the sauce and serve.

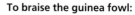

To braise the guinea fowl:

Heat the oil and the butter in a frying pan and fry the halves of guinea fowl on both sides until they are evenly light brown.

Add the garlic and onions, and cook for 6–8 minutes. Sprinkle paprika over the meat and turn several times.

After 10 minutes, add the peppers and the poultry stock, cover, and braise for a further 15–20 minutes.

Remove the meat and keep warm. Add the cream and the marjoram, and reduce the sauce to the desired consistency.

The same recipe can, of course, also be used for chicken, but it is difficult to beat the flavor of young guinea fowl.

Remove all the skin from the chicken pieces.

To make the chicken fricassee:

Melt half of the butter, add the vegetables and sweat, stirring constantly, without allowing them to color.

Season the meat with salt and pepper, place on the vegetables, and continue to cook without browning.

Dust with flour, add the remaining butter cut into small dice, and turn the meat.

Add the white wine, and cook for approximately 10 minutes until the wine has evaporated. Turn the meat again.

Pour in 2¼ cups of the prepared stock all at once, add the parsley and thyme, cover, and braise for 25 minutes.

Remove the cooked meat with a fork, place on a plate, cover with foil, and keep warm.

Strain the sauce, pressing through as much of the vegetables as possible. Heat the sauce through again.

Add the cream and reduce to approximately 1¼ cups. Then thicken with the egg yolk, and season with cayenne pepper and lemon juice.

The fricassee has fallen into disrepute because of the large quantity of flour typically used to thicken it. However, only a little flour is necessary, as the vegetables, cream and egg yolk make the sauce pleasantly thick and creamy. Indeed, it can also be cooked without any flour, as the example on the opposite page shows.

FRICASSEE WITH MORELS

Serves 4

one 4-lb roasting chicken

For the chicken stock:

½ carrot, 1 celery stick, 1 small leek

½ garlic clove, 1 bay leaf

For the fricassee:

6 tablespoons unsalted butter, ½ cup diced celery

¾ cup diced onion, 1 cup chopped leek

salt, pepper, 1½ teaspoons flour, ½ cup dry white wine

*4 sprigs fresh parsley, 2 sprigs fresh thyme,
1 cup light cream*

*1 egg yolk, ¼ teaspoon cayenne pepper,
1 teaspoon lemon juice*

Also:

2 oz morels, cooked, 8 cooked crayfish tails, chervil

Chicken fricassee
A theme with many variations

Wash the figs well, add the port, season, and poach carefully over a low heat.

Few recipes in international cuisine have been the subject of so many interpretations as this delicious chicken dish, *fricassée de poulet*. It originated in France, where the first recipe of that name, dating from 1674, is kept safely in the Bibliothèque Nationale in Paris. Since that time there have been a vast number of fricassee recipes, which have in common only the fact that they contain chicken and a sauce thickened with flour and cream. The other ingredients vary considerably.

FRICASSEE WITH FRESH FIGS

In this robust fricassee, meat and vegetables are cooked until lightly browned. Fresh tomatoes and strong seasoning, which both complement the poached figs particularly well, are then added.

Serves 4
For the figs:
8 fresh figs, 1 cup port
1 cinnamon stick, 1 clove
For the fricassee:
one 3½-lb roasting chicken, with giblets
1 carrot, 1 piece celeriac
6 tablespoons unsalted butter, ½ cup diced onion
¾ cup diced celery, 2 garlic cloves, crushed
salt, freshly ground white pepper
2 finely chopped tomatoes, ½ cup light cream

Wash the figs, dry them, and place them in a saucepan with the wine, cinnamon, and clove, and poach for 10 minutes. Quarter the figs and keep warm in the liquid. Wash the chicken and pat dry. Cut off the legs and remove the breast with the wing stumps. Skin these 4 pieces and cut in half. Chop the carcass and blanch it and the cleaned gizzard and heart in a pot with plenty of water. Drain, rinse with fresh water, and simmer gently with the carrot and the celery in 4½ cups of water for 1 hour.

Melt half of the butter in a deep frying pan and sweat the onions, celery, and garlic until lightly browned. Season the meat, add to the vegetables, and brown lightly. Scatter the remaining butter on top. Add the tomatoes and cook for 10 minutes. Strain the chicken stock into the pan, cover, and simmer for about 30 minutes until tender. Remove the meat and keep warm. Strain the sauce, pressing through as much of the vegetables as possible, and reduce to about 1 cup. Add the cream, the meat, and the quartered figs, and allow the whole dish to infuse for 5–10 minutes. Serve with noodles.

Variation: This recipe can also be used to prepare a fricassee of guinea fowl with paprika. Replace the chicken with a guinea fowl, braise 2 red peppers with it, and season the dish with 2 teaspoons of sweet paprika. Instead of the figs, serve the fricassee with white cabbage seasoned with plenty of caraway.

Wash and dry the chicken. Divide the meat into 8 pieces. Make a light stock from the carcass, heart, and gizzard; the vegetables, garlic, and bay leaf (see pages 52–3). Prepare the fricassee as described in the picture sequence to the left. After the sauce is made, add the meat, cooked morels, and crayfish tails, and heat through. Garnish with chervil.

Whole braised chicken

Whole birds are perfectly suitable for braising. Very large poultry, however, can also be braised cut into pieces. Whether cooked in an open or a closed pot, the meat stays beautifully juicy. The principle is always the same: first, rapid, even browning in hot fat, followed by the addition of the various ingredients and a good stock, then cooking over a low heat. Because of the many varied ingredients, simple accompaniments are best.

POULARDE JARDINIÈRE

Fresh summer vegetables give this braised chicken a particularly fresh taste. The vegetables also benefit from this cooking method, as they become pleasantly spicy.

Serves 4

one 3½-lb roasting chicken
1 teaspoon salt
freshly ground white pepper
½ teaspoon ground ginger
1 bouquet garni: parsley, thyme, marjoram and a little lovage
¼ cup unsalted butter
½ lb zucchini
1 lb small firm-cooking potatoes
1 fresh ear of corn
½ lb tomatoes
2¼ cups light chicken stock (see pages 52–3)
1 bunch fresh parsley
2 sprigs fresh thyme

Preheat the oven to 425°F. Wash the chicken under running water and pat dry. Season inside and out with salt, pepper, and ground ginger. Place the bouquet garni in the cavity. Truss the chicken, brush all over with butter, place in a roasting pan and brown in the oven for approximately 10 minutes. Slice the washed zucchini. Peel the potatoes, and cut into pieces if necessary. Cut the corn from the cob with a knife. Blanch, skin, and seed the tomatoes, and dice the flesh. Add the vegetables to the chicken in the roasting pan and pour in the chicken stock. Reduce the heat in the oven to 350°F and braise the chicken for approximately 20 minutes. Baste with the stock from time to time. Finely chop the parsley and the thyme, sprinkle over the chicken and continue cooking for a further 30–40 minutes, until the meat is tender.

CHICKEN BRAISED
WITH FORTY GARLIC CLOVES

This liberal approach to garlic comes from the south
of France, where rabbit is also prepared in this way.
The real secret of the recipe lies in the fact
that when garlic cloves are braised whole
and unpeeled or, at most, lightly
crushed, the chicken has a pleasantly fresh and spicy flavor, but
does not have a penetrating taste
of garlic, and the garlic does not
leave a strong odor on your
breath. Lovers of this fragrant
tuber are then free to decide
whether they want to spoon the
softly braised, very mild-tasting cloves
from the skin.

It is important that the pot remains airtight
during cooking. This is best achieved by using a
flour paste to glue the edge of the lid to the pot. A
particularly good result can be achieved in an earthenware pot or, if the edges are painted with egg yolk,
in a cast-iron pot.

Serves 4
For the paste:
2 cups flour
1 tablespoon olive oil
water
For the chicken:
one 4-lb roasting chicken
1 teaspoon salt, freshly ground white pepper
1 bouquet garni: parsley, thyme, lovage, and savory
⅓ cup finely diced carrots
½ cup finely chopped celery
½ cup olive oil
40 garlic cloves
1 bay leaf
1 sprig fresh rosemary

Place an earthenware pot in cold water for 10 minutes. To make the paste, place the flour in a bowl,
add the oil, and gradually work in sufficient water to
form a kneadable paste. Wash the chicken, carefully
pat dry, and season inside and out with salt and pepper. Place the bouquet garni in the cavity and truss
the bird. Scatter the carrots and the celery over the
bottom of the earthenware pot. Rub olive oil evenly
on all sides of the chicken, place it in the pot, and
pour on the remaining oil. Proceed as described in
the picture sequence to the right. Allow the cooked
chicken to rest for 10–15 minutes in the pot and
serve with the desired accompaniments. French
bread dipped into the juices or coated with the soft
garlic cloves tastes particularly good. A suitable
wine is a light rosé.

To braise a garlic chicken:

Preheat the oven to 350°F.
Distribute the unpeeled garlic,
bay leaf and rosemary in the
pot so that their flavors can
penetrate the meat evenly.

Form the paste into a long thin
roll, lay it evenly on the edge
of the pot, press lightly, and
place the lid on top.

Place the well-sealed pot on
the middle rack and braise for
about 1½ hours.

The chicken becomes lightly
colored when cooked in a clay
pot; it remains white when
cooked in a cast-iron pot.

Chicken and rice
Specialties with many variations

Although the combination of chicken and rice produces very simple everyday dishes, noteworthy specialties have also been developed, which, suitably refined, are among the best dishes international cuisine has to offer.

Arroz con pollo, an everyday dish in Central America.

ARROZ CON POLLO

This piquant, spicy combination of chicken and rice is a very popular dish in Mexico and throughout Central America. It is quite easy to make.

Serves 4
one 3½-lb roasting chicken
1 green pepper
½ lb tomatoes
1 large onion
1 hot chile pepper
¼ cup vegetable oil
2 garlic cloves, crushed
1 cup long-grain rice
3¼ cups light chicken stock (see pages 52–3)
1 teaspoon salt
½ teaspoon sugar
2 teaspoons freshly chopped cilantro
2 teaspoons lime juice
6–8 chorizo sausages (optional)

Wash the chicken inside and out under running water, pat dry ,and cut into 8–12 pieces. Roast the whole pepper in the oven at 425°F until the skin blisters and browns. Allow to cool slightly, then skin, remove the seeds and pith, and dice. Briefly blanch the tomatoes, remove the skin and seeds, and dice the flesh. Dice the onion. Halve the chile pepper lengthwise, remove the seeds and pith (leave them in if you like your food very spicy) and cut lengthwise into thin strips.

Heat the oil in a pan, add the crushed garlic cloves, the diced onion and pepper, and sweat gently. Mix in the tomatoes and chile pepper. Add the rice and cook, stirring constantly, until it becomes transparent. Add the chicken and the stock. Cook over a low heat until the rice and chicken are soft, about 50 minutes. Season with salt, sugar, cilantro, lime juice, and additional chile if required. If using the chorizos, slice them and add them to the dish before serving. Although they add an interesting flavor of their own, they also detract from the characteristic taste of the chicken.

JAMBALAYA

This well-known dish, in which the chicken plays just as important a role as the rice, is a Creole standard. Its name is thought to come from the French word *jambon*, meaning ham, which should be included in this dish but is often replaced by a spicy sausage. Other obligatory ingredients are freshwater crayfish, shrimp, and lobsters or oysters. In the original recipe, as it is served in New Orleans, the indigenous red swamp crayfish is included, but a fresh lobster is a good substitute.

Serves 4
one 2-lb chicken
one 1¼-lb lobster
¾ lb tomatoes
2 small chile peppers
¼ lb cooked ham
smoked bacon strips
2 tablespoons vegetable oil
½ cup diced onion
1 garlic clove, crushed
¾ cup long-grain rice
1 cup green peas
2¼ cups light chicken stock (see pages 52–3)
a few saffron threads
1 teaspoon salt, ½ teaspoon thyme

1 tablespoon lime juice
2–3 chorizo sausages
1 tablespoon chopped fresh basil leaves

Wash the chicken inside and out under running water, pat dry ,and cut into 8 pieces as described on pages 24–5. Cook the lobster for 3 minutes in boiling water and refresh in ice-cold water. Break off the tail and divide into 8 pieces. Briefly blanch the tomatoes, remove the skin and seeds, and dice the flesh. Halve the chile peppers lengthwise, carefully remove the seeds and pith, and cut the flesh lengthwise into fine strips. Cut the ham into strips.

Finely dice the bacon and brown vigorously in the oil. Add the diced onion and the crushed garlic clove, and cook for 2–3 minutes. Add the chicken pieces and the ham, and brown on all sides. Add the rice, and fry, stirring constantly, until the grains are transparent. Mix in the tomatoes and peas, and add the stock and the saffron threads. Season with the chile peppers, salt, thyme, and lime juice, and cook over a low heat until the rice and meat are soft, about 50 minutes. Add the sliced sausages and the lobster; if necessary, add more chicken stock. Leave the dish to infuse for a further 5–10 minutes. Sprinkle with basil before serving.

SQUAB RISOTTO

This recipe requires some effort if the stock is made from the carcasses, but the delicate taste certainly makes it worth while.

Serves 4
two ¾-lb squabs
salt, freshly ground white pepper
For the stock:
2 tablespoons vegetable oil
1 garlic clove, lightly crushed
¼ cup each finely diced shallots and carrots
½ cup diced celery
4½ cups water
1 bay leaf and 1 sprig fresh thyme
For the risotto:
7 teaspoons unsalted butter
2 tablespoons finely diced shallots
2 tomatoes, skinned and diced
1–2 tablespoons tomato paste
2 cups arborio rice
½ cup dry red wine

Take the breasts and legs off the squabs (see pages 24–5) and dice the meat. Season it with salt and pepper, and keep cool. To make the stock, chop the carcasses. Heat the oil in a large saucepan, add the garlic clove and the shallots, and sweat. Next, add the carcasses and the vegetables, and brown. Then add the water, bay leaf, and thyme, and simmer gently for approximately 1 hour. Then strain, allow to cool slightly, and remove the fat from the surface. Make the risotto as described in the picture sequence. Freshly grated Parmesan or *grana padano* cheese complements the taste marvelously.

Risotto with meat or giblets

Another way to combine rice and poultry

Risottos are simply an invitation to experiment. While all types of poultry can be used for risotto, not every type of rice is equally suitable. The Italian round-grain varieties are ideal, of course, but you can make a lighter risotto using American long-grain rice. A good example of this is a quail risotto. Follow the basic recipe on the opposite page, but use long-grain instead of round-grain rice. Season 4 quails with strong spices and sear them in butter until pink. Remove the meat from the bone, dice it, and mix it into the finished risotto. Sprinkle with plenty of Parmesan cheese, and serve.

To make the squab risotto:
Melt the butter and sweat the shallots in it. Add the diced meat and brown vigorously. Add the tomatoes and the tomato paste and cook for 10 minutes.

Add the rice and brown for 3–4 minutes over a high heat while stirring. Add the red wine.

When the wine has largely evaporated, add approximately 4½ cups of poultry stock. If necessary, add more water.

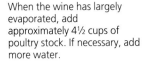

Cook uncovered until the rice is soft. From time to time, loosen the rice from the bottom of the saucepan with a spatula.

BASIC RISOTTO RECIPE
Serves 4

¼ cup unsalted butter
1 onion, finely diced
2 cups arborio rice
⅔ cup white wine
4½ cups meat broth
salt
¾ cup grated Parmesan cheese

Make the risotto as described in the picture sequence to the right. Make sure that when frying the rice, it does not color or stick to the bottom of the pot. Before serving, mix in the grated Parmesan cheese.

SAFFRON RISOTTO WITH POULTRY LIVER

Both chicken liver and turkey liver are well suited to the following recipe. The livers of fresh ducks and geese, however, have a stronger taste, which would overpower the other delicate ingredients.

Serves 4

For the saffron risotto:
1–2 tablespoons beef marrow (optional)
6 tablespoons unsalted butter, 1 onion, diced
½ garlic clove, lightly crushed
2 cups arborio rice
⅔ cup white wine
4½–5½ cups light poultry stock (see pages 52–3)
salt, about ¼ teaspoon saffron threads

For the liver:
2 tablespoons vegetable oil
1½ tablespoons unsalted butter
½ cup diced onion
1 garlic clove, lightly crushed, 1 lb diced poultry livers
salt, freshly ground white pepper
5–6 tablespoons poultry stock

Also:
¾ cup grated Parmesan cheese

Soak and dice the beef marrow, if using, and melt it with 2 tablespoons butter. Add the onion and the garlic, and continue cooking. Add the rice and cook until it is transparent. Add the white wine, reduce a little, and gradually add the stock. Season with salt, add the saffron, and cook for 12–15 minutes, stirring constantly.

To make the liver, heat the oil with 1½ tablespoons of butter, and sweat the onions and the garlic. Add the liver, sear on all sides over a high heat, season with salt and pepper, add the stock and simmer for 5–6 minutes. Stir into the finished risotto. Before serving, mix in the remaining butter and sprinkle the dish with the Parmesan cheese.

To make the risotto: Melt the butter and gently cook the onions in it. Add the rice and brown over a high heat, stirring continuously. Add the wine and reduce. Add the broth and cook for 12–15 minutes.

Coq au Riesling from Alsace. This can be made exactly as in the recipe opposite, but is no mere copy, for the Riesling gives the dish a quite special character.

COQ AU VIN WITH BURGUNDY

This recipe is a rustic version of the classic *coq au vin*, in which the chicken is not marinated. *Coq au Riesling* can also be prepared in this way, simply leaving out the tomato paste and replacing the red wine with a white Riesling.

Serves 4

one 4-lb roasting chicken
salt, freshly ground white pepper
3 slices smoked bacon
2 tablespoons vegetable oil
¼ cup unsalted butter
1 garlic clove, lightly crushed
1¼ cups diced onion
¾ cup diced carrot
3¼ cups red burgundy
2 bay leaves
1 bouquet garni: parsley, marjoram, thyme, a little lovage
2 tablespoons tomato paste
7 oz fresh mushrooms

Preheat the oven to 400°F. Wash the chicken inside and out under running water and pat dry carefully. Using poultry shears, cut out the backbone and divide the remainder into 8 pieces. Season them with salt and pepper. Dice the bacon. Heat the oil in a casserole and lightly brown the diced bacon. Skim off the fat, add the butter, and brown the chicken on all sides. Add the garlic clove, the onion and carrot, and sweat for 10 minutes, before adding the wine. Add the bay leaves, the bouquet garni, and the tomato paste, cover the pot and braise in the oven for 40–50 minutes, until the meat is tender. Add the mushrooms (cutting large ones in half) and cook, uncovered, for a further 10 minutes. Serve it as it is or pass the sauce separately. Serve with potatoes or pasta.

Braised in wine

Red wine and a fine roasting chicken

In France, the original *coq au vin* recipe calls for a one-year-old cock, but a meaty roasting chicken is also good. The most suitable wine is a robust burgundy, but other red wines can be substituted, and a different flavor can be produced using white wine.

CHICKEN BRAISED IN RED WINE

This is an élite version of the *coq au vin* recipe. Its preparation requires somewhat more time and effort than the rustic version on the opposite page.

Serves 4
one 4-lb roasting chicken
For the marinade:
1 cup diced onion
1 cup sliced celery
1/3 cup diced carrot
2 cloves
1 sprig each fresh thyme and rosemary
1 bay leaf
1 garlic clove, lightly crushed
10 peppercorns, crushed
3 1/4 cups red wine
For the chicken:
salt, freshly ground white pepper
3 teaspoons flour
2 tablespoons vegetable oil
1/4 cup unsalted butter
2 teaspoons tomato paste
1 bouquet garni: thyme, bay leaf, parsley sprig
3 1/4 cups water
For the sauce:
2/3 cup crème fraîche
salt, freshly ground white pepper
dash of lemon juice

For the garnish:
1/4 lb bacon, cut into strips
1/2 lb scallions, 7 oz mushrooms
1–2 tablespoons chopped fresh parsley

Wash the chicken and pat dry. Take off the legs and thighs. Using a pair of poultry shears, cut off the breasts with the bones underneath still attached and separate the wings. Finely chop the remainder of the carcass and the neck.

To marinate the chicken, place the pieces in a flat-bottomed dish, add the vegetables, herbs, and spices, and pour in sufficient red wine to just cover everything. Cover with foil and marinate for 2 days in the refrigerator.

Drain the chicken pieces, season with salt and pepper, and dust lightly with flour. Heat the oil and butter in a saucepan, and fry the meat until golden brown. Also fry the chopped bones. Remove the meat. Drain the vegetables from the marinade and add to the pan with the tomato paste. Cook a little, dust with the remaining flour, and fry until the flour is light brown. Separately boil the marinade and skim off any fat before adding the marinade to the pot. Add the bouquet garni, top up with water, and boil vigorously, uncovered, for 30 minutes. Return the chicken pieces to the pot and continue to simmer for approximately 30 minutes, until the meat is tender. Remove the meat again, remove the skin and bones, and cut the meat into bite-size pieces.

To make the sauce, strain the stock, pressing well to extract the juice from the vegetables and the bones. Stir in the *crème fraîche*, season with salt, pepper, and lemon juice.

To make the garnish, sweat the bacon strips, add the onions and mushrooms, and fry until lightly browned. Reheat the meat in the sauce, add the garnish, adjust the seasoning, and stir in the parsley.

The marinade enables the piquant flavor of wine, vegetables and herbs to penetrate the meat. The taste of the meat is a great deal stronger than that in the recipe on the opposite page.

Duck and red wine

Harmony in braising

There are probably as many interesting and delicious recipes for duck and red wine as there are for *coq au vin*. Every European wine-growing region that produces good red wine has its own braised chicken or duck dish, using red wine, of course. Braised poultry is popular there, however, not only because of the combination with red wine, but above all because the slow and careful braising produces tender, juicy, and well-cooked meat. There are two ways to make such a juicy duck dish: in one, the duck is marinated in the wine with the other ingredients for a fairly long time – as in the recipe on the opposite page – and in the other, the wine is added only at the time of braising, which is the case in the recipe on this page.

If the duck skin is too fatty, remove it after the duck has been braised, as during the cooking process it gives the meat a lot of flavor.

DUCK BRAISED IN RED WINE WITH THYME

Although a simple, rustic recipe, this dish demands good ingredients: a fresh duck, strong-tasting thyme, and a dry red wine.

Serves 4
one 4-lb duck
1 teaspoon salt
freshly ground white pepper
2 teaspoons roughly chopped fresh thyme
4 shallots
1 garlic clove
4½ tablespoons unsalted butter
2 tablespoons vegetable oil
1 cup finely chopped leek and celeriac
1 cup finely chopped celeriac
1 cup dry red wine
1 cup dark duck or chicken stock (see pages 50–1)
¼ cup light cream

Preheat the oven to 350°F. Wash the duck inside and out and pat dry well. Cut into 4 or 8 pieces of about equal size. You can also use the giblets if they are available. Place the duck pieces in a dish, sprinkle with salt, pepper, and the thyme, cover, and leave to marinate for about 1 hour. Finely chop the shallots and the garlic. Heat 1½ tablespoons of the butter with the oil in a large casserole and brown the duck pieces on all sides. Add the shallot, garlic, and vegetables, and cook, covered, over a medium heat for approximately 10 minutes. Add the wine and braise, uncovered, over a medium heat for 10 minutes. Add the stock, cover the pot again, and braise in the oven for approximately 1 hour. Take out the duck pieces and keep warm.

Strain the sauce, pressing through as much of the vegetables as possible. Skim the fat from the sauce and reduce to about a quarter. Beat in the cream with a wire whisk, adding further seasoning if necessary. Cut the remaining butter into bits and whisk into the sauce. Serve the duck in the sauce or serve the sauce separately. Homemade noodles and zucchini or eggplant make particularly good accompaniments.

DUCK IN RED WINE
Serves 2

one 1¾-lb duck

salt, freshly ground white pepper

For the marinade:

⅓ cup each finely chopped onion, celery, leek, and carrot

1 bay leaf

2 cloves

1 sprig fresh thyme

1 small bunch of fresh parsley

1 cup red wine

Also:

2 tablespoons vegetable oil

1 garlic clove, lightly crushed

2 tomatoes, skinned and diced

3 tablespoons unsalted butter

1½ teaspoons flour

Divide the duck into 2 legs and 2 breasts with wings. Season the meat with salt and pepper, and prepare as shown in the picture sequence below. Marinate the meat in the red wine for at least 12 hours for optimal flavor. Make a dark duck stock from the carcass as described on pages 50–1.

To make the duck in red wine:

Place the duck with the vegetables, herbs, and spices in a bowl, add the wine, and marinate for 12 hours.

Heat the oil in a deep frying pan. Add the well-dried duck pieces and brown on all sides.

Remove the vegetables from the marinade, drain, add to the meat, and cook for 4–5 minutes.

Add the marinade and braise the duck pieces, uncovered, for a further 10 minutes.

Add the garlic and tomatoes, and braise for 10 minutes.

Add 2¼ cups of duck stock, cover, and cook over a low heat for a further 20 minutes, then remove the duck pieces. Strain the sauce with the vegetables, and reduce by three quarters.

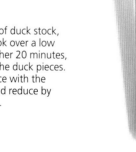

In a clean saucepan, melt the butter, stir in the flour, and cook for 1 minute. Stir in the red wine and cook to thicken. Whisk into the sauce and cook until the sauce thickens.

Whisk in the butter, add the duck pieces, and heat through. Arrange on 2 plates.

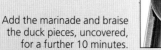

Canard à l'orange
The classic combination from France

There are two very different ways to prepare this duck dish. In one, the individual pieces of duck are braised in the liquid that later becomes the sauce; in the other, the duck is roasted whole and kept warm while the sauce is made separately. The first method is suitable for larger and older birds with flesh that is no longer quite tender. Young ducks with tender flesh are essential for the second method.

To make the sauce, the duck giblets are cut into pieces and browned in the fat with root vegetables, and stock and orange juice are poured over them. Piquant seasoning is added and the sauce is strained. Strips of orange rind are then added, and the sauce is served with the roast duck.

BRAISED DUCK WITH ORANGES.

This is a quite splendid example of the many recipes for *canard à l'orange*. It is, above all, relatively quick and easy to prepare. Although the duck does not have to be very young, the dish tastes even better if it is.

Serves 4

one 5½-lb duck
salt, freshly ground white pepper
3 tablespoons unsalted butter
¾ cup onions, ½ garlic clove
½ cup diced carrots
¼ cup diced celeriac, 1 cup diced celery
1 cup dry white wine
1 sprig fresh thyme, 1 bay leaf
2¼ cups light duck or poultry stock (see pages 52–3)
2 oranges, 2 teaspoons sugar

Wash the duck inside and out and dry carefully. Cut into 8 pieces, and season lightly with salt and pepper. Melt the butter in a large saucepan, and over a high heat sear the duck pieces on all sides until golden brown. Add the diced onions and the garlic, and sweat. Then add the diced carrots, celeriac, and celery, and braise for 10 minutes over a high heat, turning several times, before adding the wine. Add

the thyme, bay leaf, and duck stock, and braise, covered, for 70–80 minutes. Carefully brush the oranges under hot running water, and dry. Peel the skin in thin strips (without the pith) using a zester or a vegetable knife. Juice oranges, boil it with the sugar, add the pieces of zest, and cook until softened. Remove the duck pieces from the sauce and keep warm.

Strain the sauce, pushing through as much of the vegetables as possible. Reduce to 1 cup, then add 2 tablespoons of the orange liquid and 2 tablespoons of the cooked orange peel. Season to taste. Serve the sauce with the duck pieces or pass it separately.

So that the drumsticks can be cut up more easily later, remove the thighbone before searing the meat on all sides.

A simpler variation for the vegetable accompaniment: sweat the onions and the garlic only in the fat, add the pepper and braise without the sauerkraut.

Goose legs with paprika sauerkraut

A hearty braised dish

This dish tastes particularly good with smoked goose legs. Fresh goose legs are also suitable, but they must be salted. The quantity of meat does seem high at first, but allowing for the bones and the fat given off, it is just right. This recipe will serve 2 as a main course, or 4 as an appetizer.

2 cured goose legs, about 1 lb each
freshly ground white pepper
3 tablespoons vegetable oil
½ cup light poultry stock (see pages 52–3)
For the paprika sauerkraut:
½ cup diced shallots
1 garlic clove, crushed
1 each green, red and yellow pepper
1 lb sauerkraut
1 teaspoon sweet paprika, salt

Remove the thigh bones from the goose legs and pepper the meat lightly. Heat the oil in a pan and sear the legs on all sides until golden brown. Add the stock, cover, and braise for 15 minutes. Remove the legs. Add the shallots and the garlic to the cooking liquid and cook to soften. Core and seed the peppers, cut into pieces, and braise for 5 minutes. Add the sauerkraut, place the goose legs on top, cover, and braise until the meat is cooked, about 30–40 minutes. Add the paprika and salt to taste. This dish is delicious served with dumplings.

Frying and roasting

Frying and roasting are certainly the most important methods for cooking poultry, as the tender, often lightly flavored meat, particularly in the case of chicken and turkey, is enhanced by a spicy crust. Frying is used mainly for pieces of poultry, while roasting is predominantly used for whole birds. The result is similar: crisp brown skin on the outside and juicy, tender meat on the inside. Frying is often combined with roasting in preparing breast, scallops, and cutlets. Whether these pieces are dusted with flour or coated in bread crumbs beforehand does not matter, for the contact heat in the pan will cook the meat very gently in any case. For whole birds, the radiant heat in the oven is more suitable, as it is distributed all around and penetrates the meat evenly. This does mean, however, that, with a chicken for example, the delicate breast meat, which is directly under the skin, cooks more quickly than the leg and thigh meat, which have thick bones running through them. The problem is easily solved by cooking the legs further after carving the breast, and serving them later.

There are two methods for roasting heavier birds, such as duck, goose, and turkey. In the first method, the meat is browned at a high temperature, and then roasted at a lower temperature for the remainder of the cooking time. This is important in the case of goose and duck, as it draws out excess fat. In the second method, the bird is roasted at a lower temperature throughout its cooking time. This allows large poultry to cook more evenly, particularly if it is turned from time to time and basted often with the cooking juices.

A simple and delicious way to cook poultry: a good chicken, roasted with plenty of butter and fresh herbs.
The result: juicy meat and a tasty crust.

Pan-fried breasts of poultry

The breasts are particularly suitable for individual servings. Their lean meat is ideal for a healthy diet, and it can be accompanied by the most varied taste components. Pan-frying is probably the most frequently used cooking method for these tender pieces. The basic technique varies only slightly for different types of poultry, and the cooking time depends on the size and weight of the individual pieces. The breasts of the smaller types of poultry, such as the squab and guinea fowl, are always cooked whole. The large breasts of the turkey, on the other hand, are usually cut up and cooked in the form of scallops or even strips.

You can stuff poultry breasts of all sizes by cutting a pouch in them and filling it with a stuffing. In the case of large breasts or large breast halves, you can remove the attached fillet, or "oyster," slightly flatten both the breast and the fillet, place the stuffing on the breast, and the fillet on top of the stuffing. You then roll and carefully tie the meat to make sure that the stuffing does not come out during cooking. The large turkey breast is ideal for stuffing.

SQUAB BREAST WITH *FOIE GRAS* SAUCE

Serves 2
4 squab breasts with wing bones, about 3 oz each
salt, freshly ground white pepper
3 tablespoons vegetable oil
2 teaspoons unsalted butter
For the sauce:
½ cup dark poultry stock (see pages 50–1)
5½ tablespoons light cream
1 tablespoon foie gras *parfait (see pages 176–7)*

Before cooking the breasts, reduce the poultry stock for the sauce to half and add the cream. Simmer for 2–3 minutes and set the sauce aside. Cook the squab breasts as described in the picture sequence below. Bring the sauce back to a boil, mix in the *foie gras* with a whisk, add the seasoning, and remove from the heat. Arrange the sliced squab breasts on plates with the sauce.

BREAST OF GUINEA FOWL WITH SAGE

Serves 2
2 breasts of guinea fowl, 5½ oz each
salt, freshly ground white pepper
10 fresh sage leaves
3 tablespoons vegetable oil
2 teaspoons butter
For the sauce:
1 cup dark poultry stock (see pages 50–1)
½ teaspoon cornstarch

First reduce the poultry stock for the sauce to half. Cook the breasts as described in the picture sequence below. Cut the remaining 4 sage leaves into fine strips and add to the reduced stock. Thicken the sauce with the cornstarch mixed with a little water, and season. Slice the breasts, working from the end of the breast to the tip, and arrange in a fan shape. Serve with the sauce.

Preheat the oven to 350 °F. Cut around the skin on the wing bones and, using the back of the knife, carefully pull it back toward the breast meat. Season the breasts with salt and pepper. Heat the oil in a frying pan, briefly brown the meat on the skin side and turn over. Roast the meat for 6–8 minutes. Then add the butter, continue to cook the meat, and baste frequently with melted butter. Cut the breast into slices, arrange with the *foie gras* sauce and garnish with parsley.

Preheat the oven to 350 °F. Using a sharp knife, make a lengthwise cut in each guinea fowl breast to create a pouch. Season the meat with salt and pepper and place 3 sage leaves in each pouch. Heat the oil in a frying pan, brown the breasts on the skin side and turn over. Roast the meat for 10–12 minutes. Shortly before the end of the cooking time, add the butter, continue to cook the meat and baste with the melted butter. Allow the cooked breasts to rest a little, then cut and serve.

Turkey breasts are particularly suitable for stuffing with a hearty vegetable preparation, and are an attractive sight roasted whole, as shown here.

ROAST DUCK BREAST

If possible, roast the duck breasts in the oven using only the overhead heating element in order to keep the skin crispy. If the oven does not have a separate overhead heating element, brown the duck for longer on the skin side. Alternatively, broil the breasts with the skin side uppermost for the last 2–3 minutes of the cooking time.

Serves 2

2 duck breasts, 6 oz each
pinch of salt
freshly ground white pepper
3 tablespoons vegetable oil

Preheat the oven to 350°F and cook the breasts as shown in the picture sequence below.

Using a sharp knife, make diagonal cuts in the skin side of the duck breast to just above the flesh, creating a diamond pattern. Season the meat with salt and pepper. Heat the oil in a frying pan and brown the breasts on the skin side. They should be lightly colored. Place the breasts skin side down in a roasting pan and complete the cooking, using the broiler, if available, for 12–14 minutes. Allow the cooked duck breasts to rest briefly, then cut into equal slices, and arrange in a fan shape. Serve with steamed vegetables.

STUFFED TURKEY BREAST

It is somewhat unusual to cook a turkey breast whole, but, given a suitable occasion and a sufficient number of people, it is a welcome change.

Serves 4–6

1 turkey breast with wing bones, about 2½ lb
salt, freshly ground white pepper
3½ tablespoons vegetable oil
½ cup dark poultry stock (see pages 50–1)
For the stuffing:
3 oz chopped turkey meat from the leg, about ⅓ cup
¼ cup light cream, 1½ cups small broccoli flowerets
salt, freshly ground white pepper
1 tablespoon whipped cream

To make the stuffing, chill the chopped meat and the cream. In the meantime blanch the broccoli in boiling salted water, refresh with cold water, dry, and chop roughly. Place the chilled meat in a mixer, add salt and pepper, and purée finely. Gradually add the liquid cream and mix long enough to form a smooth paste. Pass the forcemeat through a fine strainer and chill. Then mix the forcemeat with the broccoli, season, and blend in the whipped cream.

Preheat the oven to 350°F. Cut a pouch into the turkey breast, as in the example of the guinea fowl on the opposite page, insert the forcemeat, and sew up. Heat the oil in a frying pan, season the breast, brown it on the skin side, and turn it over. Place the breast in a roasting pan and cook in the oven for 50–60 minutes. Add a little stock from time to time to prevent the particles on the bottom of the pan from burning. Remove the kitchen string, allow the breast to rest for a few minutes, then carve.

ROAST TURKEY LIVER
WITH POTATO AND LEEK

Of the livers of all gallinaceous poultry, turkey liver has the strongest flavor and therefore goes well with robust vegetables such as leek.

Serves 4

½ lb turkey liver, about 1¾ cups

1 teaspoon clarified butter, 1 teaspoon unsalted butter, salt, freshly ground white pepper

5½ tablespoons dark poultry stock (see pages 50–1)

For the vegetables:

2–3 leeks, 10 oz firm-cooking potatoes, such as Yukon Gold

3½ oz. cèpe mushrooms

1 cup poultry velouté (see pages 64–5)

2 teaspoons unsalted butter, 1 shallot, finely chopped

salt, freshly ground white pepper

pinch of nutmeg

1 tablespoon whipped cream

To make the vegetables, clean the leeks, cut into ¼- inch slices and blanch. Boil the potatoes in their skins, peel, and slice. Clean and slice the cèpes. Heat the velouté in a saucepan, and add the leek and potatoes. Brown the cèpes and the shallot in the butter and add to the vegetables. Bring to a boil, and season with salt, pepper, and nutmeg. Keep warm.

Wash the turkey liver. Heat the clarified butter in a frying pan and fry the liver evenly. Add the fresh butter, allow to foam, continue to cook briefly, and season. Remove the liver. Degrease the pan with the poultry stock and reduce. Stir the whipped cream into the vegetables, and serve. Slice the liver, arrange on plates, and pour the sauce on top.

FRIED CUBES OF *FOIE GRAS* OF DUCK
WITH ASPARAGUS SALAD

Serves 4

½ lb duck foie gras

salt, freshly ground white pepper

1 tablespoon flour, 1 egg

1½ cups fresh brioche crumbs, 2 cups fresh bread crumbs

5½ tablespoons vegetable oil

For the salad:

1 lb white asparagus

salt, 1½ teaspoons sugar, 1 lemon slice

For the vinaigrette:

2 tablespoons raspberry vinegar, salt, freshly ground white pepper

½ cup olive oil

Also:

1 tomato

½ tablespoon finely chopped fresh chives

Quick fried liver

When fried, livers from poultry that has been reared naturally behave differently from those of force-fed birds, which melt easily because of their higher fat content. For this reason it is important to chill them well before use, and remove them from the refrigerator immediately before cooking. In this way they become crisp on the outside, while remaining soft and tender on the inside.

To make the salad, peel the asparagus, and cook in boiling water with a pinch of salt, the sugar, and the lemon slice until *al dente*. Drain and refresh with cold water. To make the vinaigrette, mix the vinegar with salt and pepper, add the oil, and stir well. Cut the asparagus tips into 2-inch lengths, halve lengthwise, and slice the ends. Marinate the asparagus in the vinaigrette. Blanch the tomatoes, skin, quarter, seed, dice, and add to the vinaigrette. Shortly before serving, sprinkle with the chives.

Cut the liver into 1-inch thick slices, then into strips, and finally into cubes. Season these with salt and pepper, cover in flour, dip in the beaten egg, and coat with the mixed bread crumbs. Press the coating firmly into place and chill the liver again briefly. Heat the oil in a frying pan and fry the pieces of liver on all sides only briefly, until lightly browned. Arrange the liver cubes with the asparagus salad and serve immediately.

To fry *foie gras* of goose:
Cut the liver into slices, removing any tiny veins. Season the slices with salt and pepper and fry on both sides in a hot pan, without fat, until they are lightly colored.

FRIED *FOIE GRAS* WITH A CONFIT OF SHALLOT

Fried *foie gras* is unparalleled in flavor.

Serves 4

½ lb goose foie gras
For the confit:
6–7 shallots
1 teaspoon unsalted butter
1 sprig fresh thyme
1 cup strong red wine
¼ cup port
½ cup dark poultry stock (see pages 50–1)
salt, freshly ground white pepper
Also:
2 endives

Cut the liver into 8 equal slices, and chill. To make the confit, peel the shallots, cut into rings, and sweat briefly in the butter. Add the thyme, red wine, and port, and reduce over a low heat until a little remains. Add the poultry stock, continue to simmer until the shallots are cooked and the stock has reduced by half, then season with salt and pepper. Fry the *foie gras* as described on the right, but make sure that it remains soft in the center. Arrange the confit of shallots with the clean endives and add the liver slices.

TURKEY BREAST CORDON BLEU

Ideally, cut the individual portions from a whole turkey breast, as this is easier than cutting pouches in turkey scallops.

Serves 2

| one ¾-lb turkey breast |
| salt, freshly ground white pepper |
| 2 slices cooked ham |
| 2 slices Emmenthal cheese |
| flour, 1 egg, and bread crumbs for coating |
| 3½ tablespoons vegetable oil |
| 2 teaspoons unsalted butter |

Cut the meat against the grain. If cutting 2 portions from a whole turkey breast, cut the pouch for stuffing at the same time: slice partway through the meat at half the thickness of the portion, then make another slice, this time all the way through, to separate the portion from the breast. Fill the pouches and coat with bread crumbs as shown in the picture sequence to the left. Heat the oil in a frying pan and fry the meat on both sides for a total of 3–4 minutes. Shortly before the end of the cooking time, add the butter, allow it to foam, and continue to cook.

Drain the breasts on paper towels. Serve with potato purée and bundles of green beans wrapped in bacon. Sprinkle with drops of lemon juice, if desired.

Turkey *cordon bleu*:
Season the meat pouches and place 1 slice of ham and 1 slice of cheese in each. Coat with flour, beaten egg, and bread crumbs, pressing the crumbs into place.

STUFFED CHICKEN CUTLETS

Serves 4

| two 2-lb chickens |
| about ⅓ cup diced chicken breast |
| salt, freshly ground pepper |
| 5½ tablespoons light cream |
| 1 tablespoon whipped cream |
| ¼ cup shelled pistachios |
| 1 oz black truffles from a jar |
| 1½ tablespoons vegetable oil |

Bone the chickens as described in the picture sequence below, then chill. Finely dice the additional chicken breast and chill thoroughly. Place the diced meat in a food processor, add salt and pepper, purée, and gradually add the cream. Press this forcemeat through a fine strainer, adjust the seasoning, and blend in the whipped cream. Halve the pistachios, slice the truffles, and mix both into the forcemeat. Season the legs and breasts with salt and pepper. Spread the forcemeat onto the legs as described below and cover with the breasts.

Preheat the oven to 350°F. Take 2 large pieces of skin from the chicken carcasses, tightly wrap each portion of stuffed meat in one, and secure with toothpicks or skewers. Brown the cutlets all over in hot oil in a frying pan, then place them in a roasting pan and cook in the oven for 12–14 minutes.

To make the cutlets:

Cut off the legs and breasts. Detach the wings from the breasts, and carefully skin the breasts.

Skin the legs, uncover and clean the lower leg bones, and remove the thigh bones.

Season the legs, coat with forcemeat, place a breast on top of each, with the tip pointing toward the bone, and cook.

Remove the cutlets from the oven, allow to rest briefly, and then slice.

Stuffed and fried or roasted
A creative way to cook the finest cuts of poultry

For these recipes, you need the best quality poultry . Then the effort required for such a time-consuming preparation — not to mention the cost of such fine ingredients as black truffles and *foie gras* — is worthwhile.

GUINEA FOWL CUTLETS WITH *FOIE GRAS*

These cutlets made from the breast and leg with a melt-in-the-mouth filling of *foie gras* are a very special delicacy.

Serves 4
two ¾-lb young guinea fowls
salt, freshly ground white pepper
2 oz foie gras
¼ cup vegetable oil
For the sauce:
1 tablespoon mustard seeds
1¼ cups apple juice
1 cup dark poultry stock (see pages 50–1)
½ teaspoon cornstarch
salt, freshly ground white pepper

Cut the guinea fowls in half carefully and remove the skin from each half in one piece. Prepare the cutlets as shown in the picture sequence below. Then wrap each piece of meat tightly in a piece of skin and secure with toothpicks or skewers. Heat the oil in a frying pan and brown the meat first on the breast side, then turn and complete the cooking on the leg side.

To make the sauce, bring the apple juice to a boil with the mustard seeds and simmer for 15 minutes. Heat the poultry stock in another saucepan and reduce to about half. Strain the apple juice through a cloth, and add the mustard seeds to the poultry stock. Stir in the cornstarch mixed with a little water and salt and pepper.

Cutlets stuffed with *foie gras* of goose:

Remove the thigh bone with a sharp knife, and season the meat with salt and pepper.

Cut the *foie gras* into 4 rectangles of equal thickness and place 1 on each thigh.

Place the breasts on top so that the tip of the breast points toward the lower part of the leg and press firmly.

Preheat the oven to 350°F. After browning the cutlets, place them in a roasting pan and cook in the oven for 12–15 minutes. Remove, allow to rest briefly, slice, arrange on plates, and serve with the mustard seed sauce. Serve with tagliatelle and baby vegetables.

To carve the guinea fowl:

Allow the roast guinea fowl to rest for 5 minutes. Remove the string. Make an incision between the breast and the leg.

Cut deep enough to reveal the hip joint. Push the leg sideways and cut through the joint.

Detach the wings underneath the breast. Cut into the breasts carefully along the breastbone.

Remove the breasts from the carcass. Point the blade toward the carcass so as not to damage the meat.

Cut the breasts into even slices, working from the start of the wing toward the tip of the breast.

Allow the remaining butter to foam in the roasting pan and continue to cook the legs in the oven for 8–10 minutes.

Make an incision in the legs between the drumstick and the thigh, and cut through the knee joint.

Take out the upper and lower leg bones, and slice the meat.

To roast the guinea fowl:
Preheat the oven to 350°F. Season and truss the guinea fowl. Brown the breast side in the oil in a roasting pan. Turn onto the back, brush the breasts and legs with 2 tablespoons soft butter. Roast the guinea fowl for 40–50 minutes. Baste several times with the cooking juices.

ROAST GUINEA FOWL, SERVED IN TWO COURSES
Serves 2–4

one 3½-lb guinea fowl

salt, freshly ground white pepper

¼ cup vegetable oil

3 tablespoons unsalted butter

Cook the guinea fowl as described in the picture sequence to the left. After roasting, allow the meat to rest for 5 minutes, so that not too much juice escapes during carving. Serve the breasts as a first course with vegetables, garnishes, and a cream sauce. Serve the legs and wings as a main course with a delicate bouquet of salad and the natural meat juices.

Roasted whole and served separately

Some parts of the bird take longer to cook

Roasting a whole bird has its advantages. The roast is crispy on the outside and juicy within, because the skin and the outer layers cook quickly in the dry heat, forming a protective layer under which the juices conduct the heat inward and cook the meat. During roasting, the bones also impart flavor to the meat, giving it its unmistakable taste.

Whole roasted poultry is always an impressive dish, particularly when it is carved in front of the guests. A bird can also be served in two courses, as shown in the example of the guinea fowl on the opposite page. This is ideal in the case of larger types of poultry, for, as a rule, the breasts are ready before the legs and would become dry by the end of the total cooking time. The shorter roasting time for the breasts and the separate continued roasting of the legs produces a good result. In the case of smaller poultry, such as quail or squab, the breasts and legs are cooked for the same length of time.

ROAST SQUABS WITH TRUFFLE SAUCE

Serves 2

two ¾-lb squabs
salt, freshly ground white pepper
3 tablespoons vegetable oil, 2 teaspoons butter
For the sauce:
2½ tablespoons truffle stock
1 cup dark poultry stock (see pages 50–1)
2 teaspoons cold unsalted butter, 1¼ oz sliced truffles

Preheat the oven to 350°F. Season the squabs with salt and pepper, and truss into shape. Heat the oil in a frying pan, briefly brown the squabs on the breast side, and turn over. Place them in a roasting pan and roast for 15–18 minutes. About 5 minutes before the end of this time, add the butter and baste the squabs with it several times. Allow to rest for 3–4 minutes and continue as described below. To make the sauce, reduce the truffle stock until a little remains, add the poultry stock and reduce to a third. Stir in the cold butter and add the truffles.

To test whether the meat is fully cooked, pierce the thickest part of the thigh with a skewer. The meat is done when the juices run clear, with no trace of pink.

To carve the squab and make the truffle sauce:

Using a knife, make an incision in the skin between the breast and the leg, and detach the legs at the hip joint.

Make an incision into the breasts along the breastbone and detach from the carcass. Cut through the wing bones at the joint.

Line a small strainer with a cloth, insert the squab carcasses, and squeeze hard.

Bring the truffle sauce to the boil and thicken with the juice from the carcasses.

Arrange the squab pieces on polenta, top with the truffle sauce, and garnish with truffle slices.

Basil, Calvados, and apples: A harmonious combination.

BASIL CHICKEN WITH CALVADOS AND APPLES

Serves 4
one 3¾-lb roasting chicken
salt
3 tart apples
12 fresh basil leaves
½ cup Calvados
¼ cup unsalted butter
For the sauce:
½ cup dry cider
½ cup crème fraîche
salt, freshly ground white pepper

Wash the chicken thoroughly, pat dry, and season inside and out with salt. Peel one of the apples and cut into slivers. Stuff the stomach cavity of the chicken with 5 basil leaves and the apple slivers, close it, and place the bird in a roasting pan. Halve 5 basil leaves. Carefully lift the skin of the chicken breast and legs, and place the halved basil leaves under it. Pour half of the Calvados over the chicken and marinate for 30 minutes, basting it several times with the Calvados that runs off.

Preheat the oven to 450°F. Melt the butter, drizzle three-quarters of it evenly over the chicken, and place the bird in the oven. Peel and halve the remaining apples, remove the core, and place half a basil leaf in each hollow. Turn the chicken after 35 minutes, surround with the apple halves, and sprinkle with the remaining Calvados and the remaining melted butter. Cover and cook for a further 20 minutes. Arrange the chicken and the apples on a platter, cover, and keep warm. Degrease the roasting pan with the cider, strain, and skim off the fat. Mix in the *crème fraîche*, reduce a little, and adjust the seasoning. Serve the chicken and the sauce separately.

Cooking times for poultry			
Type of poultry	Weight (lb)	Cooking time (minutes)	
		Roasting in the oven	
		on the rack	in a roasting container
Small chicken	1½–2½	45–60	45–60
Large chicken	2½–4	60–75	60–70
Young turkey	5½–7½	90–180	120–180
Duckling	2½–5½	75–105	105–120
Muscovy duck	2½–6½	80–120	80–120
Goose	6½–13	150–180	150–180
Quail	¼–⅓	30–40	30–40
Guinea fowl	2¼–4	60–75	60–70
Squab	⅔–¾	40–50	40–50

It is particularly important that poultry is cooked thoroughly to kill any salmonella bacteria. The table gives a guide to roasting times for the most important types of poultry. Alternatively, you can check the core temperature with a thermometer, which should show at least 176°F, and preferably 195°F.

A beautifully presented roast chicken should continue to look good when it is being carved. The right tools for this are a two-pronged fork and a very sharp carving knife. Follow the directions below for an attractive, neat job.

Carving a roast chicken:

Detach the wings: Lay the chicken on its back, insert the fork into the wing and hold firmly; cut through the joint.

Remove the legs: Push the leg away from the body with the fork, without piercing it; cut into the skin, then cut through the joint.

Divide the legs into thighs and drumsticks: Hold the drumstick firmly with the fork, locate the joint and cut through it with the knife.

Cut the breast off in slices: Insert the fork into the backbone to hold the chicken securely; cut off even slices.

Alternatively, take the breast off in one piece, hold it with the fingers, and slice evenly.

Carved or halved

Two easy ways to roast poultry

Both of these methods are perfect for preserving the flavor of meat and bones. Cutting up roast poultry is not difficult if you follow the directions in the picture sequence on the opposite page. A small chicken roasted in halves can serve two.

POLLO ALLA ROMANA

This oven-roasted dish is quick and easy to make and can be varied in many ways by adding vegetables, different herbs and spices, or by using a guinea fowl instead of a chicken.

Serves 2

one 3-lb chicken
1 garlic clove, chopped
salt, freshly ground white pepper
3 tablespoons chopped fresh herbs: sage, parsley, rosemary, and marjoram
grated zest of 1/2 lemon
3 tablespoons olive oil
4 slices bacon
1/2 cup dry white wine
10 oz tomatoes
1 1/4 cups diced scallions

Wash the chicken, pat dry, and halve lengthwise. Mix the chopped garlic, salt, pepper, herbs and lemon zest together. Prepare the chicken as shown in the first two pictures in the sequence above. Then preheat the oven to 450°F. Place the chicken in a greased ovenproof dish, brown briefly in the oven, add the wine and return to the oven for 15 minutes.

Meanwhile, skin and dice the tomatoes. Add to the chicken with the scallions and complete the cooking, as shown above.

To make the *pollo alla romana*:

Spread two-thirds of the herb mixture evenly on the inside of the chicken. During cooking the flavor penetrates the meat.

Sprinkle the herb mixture also on the outsides of the chicken halves, sprinkle with drops of oil, place the bacon strips on top, and place in a dish.

Add the tomatoes and the scallions, reduce the heat to 350°F and cook for a further 30 minutes.

"Freshness is best" is the motto of this Italian poultry seller. His wares walk merrily around the market stall.

Pollo alla romana: the herbs, garlic, and tomatoes give it its typical flavor, while the bacon adds spiciness.

Delicate stuffings
Two ways to stuff a chicken

The stomach cavity is the most usual place for stuffing, but stuffing under the skin also has its advantages: the poultry and the stuffing cook more quickly and evenly, and the sensitive breast meat is protected by the stuffing, so it stays pleasantly juicy.

CHICKEN WITH CHEESE STUFFING

Serves 4
two 1½-lb chickens
salt, freshly ground pepper
For the stuffing:
1½ stale rolls, 2 tablespoons unsalted butter
⅓ cup diced onion, 1 garlic clove, crushed
2 slices bacon, finely diced
½ cup diced chicken liver
½ cup milk, 1 egg
3 tablespoons chopped fresh basil, thyme, and parsley
salt, freshly ground pepper
1 cup finely diced Gruyère cheese
melted butter for roasting

Season the chickens with salt and pepper. Dice half a roll and brown it in half of the butter. Heat the remaining butter, and sweat the onions, garlic, and bacon. Add the chicken liver and continue to cook for about 1 minute. Make the stuffing and prepare the chickens as shown below. Preheat the oven to 400°F and roast the chickens for 30 minutes. Sprinkle on the herbs and melted butter, and continue roasting for 10–15 minutes.

To stuff the stomach cavity:

Remove the crust from a roll, cut the bread into slices, pour the lukewarm milk on top, and leave to soak.

Place the stuffing in the chickens, but do not stuff them too full. Coat the skin with melted butter.

Add the toasted cubes of bread and the cheese, and mix together well.

Use toothpicks, skewers, or a needle and string to close the opening carefully. Tie the legs together at the joint.

Add the egg, half the herbs, and the mixture of onions, bacon, and liver. Mix together and season with salt and pepper.

After roasting, allow the chickens to rest for 10 minutes, then halve lengthwise and serve a half to each person.

To stuff under the skin:

Place the prepared ingredients for the stuffing in a bowl and mix to a soft paste.

Cut open the chicken along the back, place on a chopping board with the cut side downward, and press flat.

Starting at the neck and moving your fingers toward the rump, loosen the skin from the flesh without tearing it.

CHICKEN WITH SPINACH STUFFING

Cut open, pressed flat, and stuffed under the skin, the chicken cooks quickly and evenly, and is easy to serve.

Loosen the skin on one side as far as the lower leg, then repeat the procedure on the other side.

Serves 4
one 3½-lb chicken
For the stuffing:
3 slices bacon, finely diced
8½ tablespoons unsalted butter
¾ cup finely diced poultry liver
2¾ cups bread without crusts
2½ cups fresh spinach
1 egg
2 tablespoons chopped fresh parsley
1 teaspoon salt
freshly ground pepper
pinch of nutmeg
For roasting:
butter for brushing

Using a spoon, insert the stuffing between the skin and the flesh, and spread it well. To close, fold down the neck skin.

Pierce the loose skin between the legs with the tip of the knife and cut a slit ¾ inch long.

To make the stuffing, sweat the bacon and shallots in 1½ tablespoons of butter. Add the poultry liver and cook briefly, then remove from the heat and allow to cool. Brown half of the diced bread in about ¼ cup of the butter. Wash the spinach and remove the stalks. Blanch the spinach in boiling salted water, allow to drain briefly, then chop finely. Whisk or beat the remaining butter until frothy, then mix in the egg. Add the parsley. Complete the stuffing as shown in the picture sequence to the right, and stuff the chicken with it. Preheat the oven to 350°F. Brush the chicken with butter and roast for 1½–2 hours, until done.

Push the ends of the legs through the slit. Push the stuffing with your hands so that it is distributed evenly, and return the chicken to its original shape.

Allow the chicken to rest for 10 minutes after roasting. Cut first along the middle of the breast, then detach the legs, and serve.

The big birds

Roast large birds whole for full flavor

Individual pieces of poultry can be prepared in many delightful ways, but the characteristic taste of the bird itself really comes out only when it is roasted whole. Insulated by the skin, the meat develops its inherent flavor, enhanced by that of the bones, in the optimum way during roasting. Duck and goose, in particular, are extremely popular when many portions are required. Although good, tender, fresh young geese are available only in the fall, fresh ducks — as well as frozen ducks and geese — are for sale throughout the year.

DUCK IN CHERRY SAUCE

Serves 2–4
one 5½-lb duck
salt, freshly ground white pepper
2 sprigs fresh thyme
2¼ cups duck or chicken stock (see pages 52–3)
For the sauce:
1 cup canned or bottled stoned sour cherries
½ cup dry red wine
pinch of ground cloves
pinch of cinnamon
2 tablespoons light cream
1 tablespoon ground almonds

Preheat the oven to 400°F. Wash the duck under cold running water, and pat dry inside and out with paper towels. Cut off all visible fat. Mix the salt and pepper, and rub vigorously into the duck both inside and out. Place the thyme in the stomach cavity. Place the duck in a roasting pan and roast for 60–70 minutes. Baste with the hot poultry stock as required. Halfway through the cooking time turn the duck over. To make the skin crispy, brush it several times with salted water.

To make the sauce, drain the sour cherries and reserve the liquid. Purée half the cherries. Heat the reserved juice with the wine, and boil down for 2–3 minutes. Season with cloves and cinnamon, add degreased cooking juices from the duck, and reduce the sauce by about a third. Add the whole and the puréed sour cherries, heat, and mix in the cream and the almonds. The duck is cooked if the juices run clear when a skewer is stuck into the thickest part.

Before carving allow the duck to rest for 10 minutes. Serve with cherry sauce and potato croquettes.

Trussing to roast whole

Using a goose as an example, the pictures below demonstrate how such a large bird can be trussed so that it retains its shape during roasting. Although the bird can be trussed using a needle and thread, here we show you how to do it simply by tying it with string. The advantage of this technique is that it does not pierce the meat and therefore none of the juices escape.

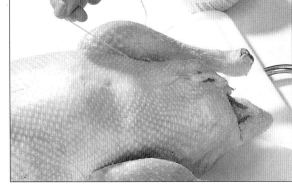

4 To secure the wings, place the goose on its breast, pass the string under the end of the wings, and cross it over on the back.

For crisp skin, mix equal parts of honey and stock, and brush it on repeatedly during roasting.

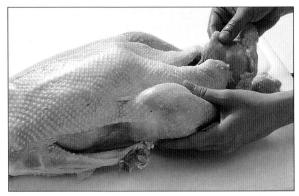

1 Carefully remove the visible abdominal fat as completely as possible. Season inside with salt and pepper, and stuff if desired.

5 Now secure the legs. Lay the goose on its back again and bring the string up from underneath between the legs and the body.

2 Close the abdominal opening. If the goose has not been stuffed, use a toothpick or skewer; if it has been stuffed, sew up the opening.

6 Cross the string over above the skewered opening and pull it through under the ends of the legs, keeping it as tight as possible.

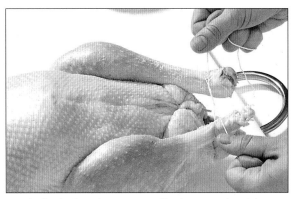

3 To close the neck opening, pull the neck skin back over the backbone and attach it to the skin underneath with a toothpick.

7 Finally, tie the string on top, pulling it more or less tight, depending on how close together the ends of the legs are intended to be.

Using a meat thermometer it is possible to find out exactly how well cooked the individual parts of the duck are. The bird should reach a core temperature of 176–195°F, while 165–170°F is sufficient for the precooked stuffing.

DUCK WITH LIVER STUFFING

The combination of bread and duck livers produces a particularly light, intensely flavored stuffing. The other giblets can also be added: simply remove the skin from the gizzard, dice all the giblets, fry them in butter until half-cooked, and add them to the stuffing.

Serves 2–4
one 4-lb duck
For the stuffing:
2 stale rolls
½ cup light poultry stock (see pages 52–3)
1¼ cups diced duck liver, ½ cup diced onions
2 tablespoons vegetable oil, 1 egg
½ garlic clove, crushed
½ teaspoon salt
freshly ground white pepper
2 teaspoons chopped fresh herbs: parsley, marjoram and sage

Wash the duck inside and out under cold running water and carefully pat dry. Make the liver stuffing and roast the duck as described in the picture sequence below.

Preheat the oven to 350°F. Use a grater to remove the crust from the rolls. Slice the rolls and place in a dish. Heat the stock and pour it on top. Heat the oil, lightly fry the onions, add the livers and sear. Add the mixture to the rolls, and mix with the egg, spices, and herbs. Stuff the stomach cavity of the duck evenly; do not fill too full, as the stuffing will expand during cooking. Close the opening. Roast the duck for about 2 hours, or until crisp and brown.

Stuffed duck

Three examples of fine stuffings

The stuffings shown here are intended to complement the flavor of the duck, but they can also be used for lean poultry. If the duck has been boned before stuffing, as shown on pages 40–1, it is particularly easy to carve after cooking. Remember, too, that stuffing adds to the cooking time of poultry, so be sure to test the thigh to see that the bird is thoroughly cooked.

DUCK WITH MEAT STUFFING

Serves 4
one 7-lb duck, boned
salt, freshly ground white pepper
For the stuffing:
2 rolls, 7 teaspoons unsalted butter
1 cup light poultry stock, 1 cup ground pork
½ cup diced onion, 1 garlic clove, crushed
1 teaspoon grated lemon zest
3 tablespoons chopped fresh herbs: parsley, chive, lovage, sage and rosemary
salt, freshly ground white pepper, 1 egg
For roasting:
2 tablespoons vegetable oil, 1 bouquet garni

Wash the duck inside and out under running water and carefully pat dry. To make the stuffing, remove the crusts from the rolls, cut the bread into small dice, and brown lightly in hot butter. Heat the

DUCK STUFFED WITH POULTRY FORCEMEAT

Serves 4

one 5½-lb duck, boned

2 tablespoons vegetable oil

For the stuffing:

8 oz chicken breast

salt

freshly ground white pepper

1 cup well-chilled light cream

3 tablespoons whipped cream

1 duck liver

1 duck heart

¼ cup unsalted butter

5 slices lightly toasted bread, without crusts

¾ cup diced carrots

1¼ cups diced zucchini

1 small bunch fresh parsley

Perfect for carving: A boned, stuffed duck can be cut in even slices right up to the leg bones.

Wash the duck inside and out under running water and pat dry. To make the stuffing, finely dice the chicken breast and chill well. Season the meat with salt and pepper, purée finely in a food processor, gradually adding the well-chilled light cream. Place the forcemeat in a bowl on ice and stir to a smooth paste. Chill again briefly, then rub through a strainer, and blend in the whipped cream.

Now prepare the other ingredients for the forcemeat. Finely dice the liver and heart, sear them in 1 teaspoon of butter, and drain. Finely dice the toast. Heat the remaining butter in a frying pan and fry the toast until golden brown. Remove and drain on paper towels. Blanch the carrots and zucchini separately in boiling salted water and refresh with cold water. Finely chop the parsley and reserve 1 tablespoon. Add these other ingredients to the forcemeat and carefully mix in. Stuff the duck with the forcemeat and close the opening.

Preheat the oven to 350°F. Heat the oil in a roasting pan on top of the stove and briefly sear the duck on both sides of the breast. Roast the duck, breast-side up, for 50–60 minutes. If the duck is very fatty, pierce the skin several times with a needle or skewer before roasting, so that the fat can drain out more easily. After about 10 minutes, pour on some water so that the exuded fat does not burn. Repeat this process 2–3 times before the end of the cooking time. When the duck is cooked, remove the string, and allow the bird to rest for a few minutes. Sprinkle the duck with the reserved parsley, and carve.

stock, pour it onto the bread, and allow to infuse for 5 minutes. Work the remaining ingredients into a soft meat paste and add plenty of seasoning. Stuff and roast the duck as shown below.

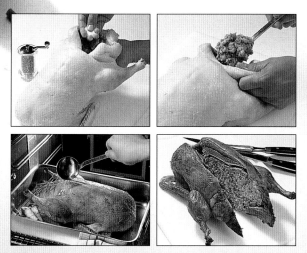

Preheat the oven to 350°F. Season the cavity of the duck with salt and pepper. Add the stuffing and distribute evenly, bearing in mind that the stuffing will expand during cooking. Close the opening as shown on pages 38–9. Brush the duck with oil and place in a roasting pan with the bouquet garni. Roast for approximately 2 hours until crisp and brown. Baste with the cooking juices from time to time. Allow to rest briefly and cut lengthwise to serve.

To peel fresh chestnuts: Cut a cross into the peel with a sharp knife and roast in the oven at 425°F for about 10 minutes, until the peel springs open. Remove while still hot.

THE CLASSIC ROAST GOOSE

In fall, when fresh, young geese come onto the market, the chestnuts are ripe and can be used to make a traditional stuffing. The method described here can also be used to roast any large poultry.

Serves 4–6

one 8-lb goose, with heart and liver
salt, freshly ground white pepper
For the stuffing:
1¼ lb fresh chestnuts, 2 apples
1 stale roll, ¼ cup water
¼ cup white wine
7 teaspoons unsalted butter
1 tablespoon finely chopped shallots
1 teaspoon salt, freshly ground white pepper
2 tablespoons freshly chopped fresh herbs: parsley, thyme and marjoram
For basting:
¼ cup soft unsalted butter, ½ cup beer mixed with 1 teaspoon salt

Wash the goose inside and out, pat dry, and season inside and out with salt and pepper. To make the stuffing, peel and finely chop the chestnuts. Peel the apples, cut into pieces, remove the core, and finely dice the flesh. Dice the roll and sprinkle with water and wine. Finely dice the heart and the liver. Melt the butter in a frying pan. First lightly brown the heart, add the shallots, and then the liver, and sear only very briefly. In a bowl mix the chestnuts, the apples, the roll, and salt and pepper. Add more salt if necessary.

Preheat the oven to 400°F. Stuff the goose and sew up the opening or close it with wooden skewers. Brush the goose with the softened butter, place it breast-side down in a roasting pan, and put it in the oven. When the breast has browned, turn the goose over and continue to roast, from time to time basting alternately with the salted beer (this makes the skin nice and crispy) and the dripping. Cook for a total of about 2½ hours, testing the thigh to be sure the meat is done. Skim the fat from the cooking juices, and serve the goose with red cabbage.

Carving a goose

A technique that can also be used for duck

Carving a goose or a duck differs from carving lean poultry — chicken and turkey — because these birds are anatomically quite different. Goose and duck have a very firm skin and tough sinews, and the bone can be severed only by applying considerable force. Before carving, always allow the fat to drain off; tilt the bird, so that the fat can run out of the stomach cavity. In addition, as for all large roasts, let the fully cooked roast rest for at least 10 minutes, wrapped in foil if possible, so that the meat juices are not lost during carving.

If the bird is to be carved in the kitchen, where no one is watching, you can use your hands to help. At the table, however, use a carving knife and fork, or even poultry shears, and try to avoid touching the meat with your hands. It is usually only the meaty parts (legs, breasts, and wings) that are detached at the table. The carcass, which has relatively little meat, can be carved in the kitchen.

Remove the legs: Take hold of the leg bone between the prongs of the meat fork. Twist the fork slightly to hold the bone firmly. Cut along the body as far as the joint. Move the bone with a slight twisting movement of the fork and sever the joint with the knife.

Slice the breast: Firmly hold the goose with the meat fork and cut the breast into even slices parallel to the breastbone. Alternatively, remove the breast from the carcass and cut into thick slices diagonally, at right angles to the grain of the meat.

With stuffed geese the carving method shown opposite can be used. When the breast has been removed, cut open along the breastbone with a pair of poultry shears, push the rib cage apart and take out the stuffing.

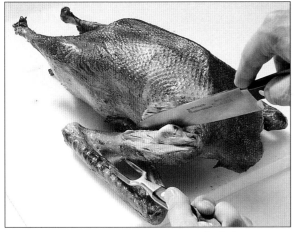

Remove the wings: Place the goose with its back down on a carving board. Pierce the wing with a meat fork and pull slightly away from the body. Take a sharp knife and, by moving the wing carefully, determine the location of the joint. Cut through the skin first, then through the joint.

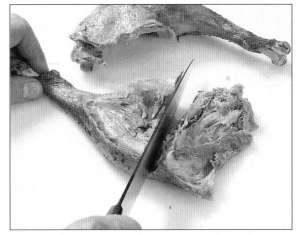

Cut up the legs: Hold the end of the bone firmly with the fingers, find the joint by moving the leg, and sever with the knife. The remaining parts of the goose can easily be divided into portions using a pair of poultry shears.

TURKEY WITH CORN PATTIES

Large poultry roasts do not have to be served only on traditional holidays. Here is a recipe that will make a celebration out of any meal.

Serves 4–6

one 7–8-lb baby turkey with giblets
1 tablespoon salt, 1 bundle fresh herbs
¼ cup clarified butter
½ lb soup vegetables
2¼ cups light poultry stock (see pages 52–3)
1 tablespoon tomato paste
1 slice pumpernickel bread, finely chopped
1½ tablespoons port, salt
For the corn patties:
2 cups cornflakes, ½ cup cooked corn
2 eggs, salt, ¼ cup clarified butter

Wash the turkey inside and out under cold running water and carefully pat dry. Season inside and out with salt, and place the herbs in the stomach cavity. Wash the giblets and set aside. Heat the clarified butter in a roasting pan on the stove and briefly sear the turkey on all sides. Lay it on the breast side.

Preheat the oven to 350°F. Wash the soup vegetables, chop finely, and add to the roasting pan with the giblets. Place the roasting pan on the lowest rack of the oven. When the vegetables and turkey begin to brown, turn the turkey over and cook for at least 2 hours. Heat the stock, stir in the tomato paste, mix it with the cooking juices, and use to baste the turkey repeatedly. At the end of the cooking time check that the turkey is done by piercing the thickest part of the legs with a skewer; if clear juices run out, the turkey is fully cooked.

Take the turkey from the roasting pan and keep warm. Strain the cooking juices into a small saucepan, pressing hard on the vegetables to release their juices. Degrease the sauce as desired, bring back to a boil, add the pumpernickel and reduce. Strain the sauce, and add port and salt.

To make the corn patties crumble the cornflakes and mix with the corn, eggs and salt. Heat the butter in a frying pan. For each patty, place 1–2 tablespoons of the mixture in the pan, using a spoon to shape it, and fry for 2–3 minutes on each side until golden brown. Arrange the turkey on a warmed platter with the corn patties. Serve the sauce separately.

Celebrate with turkey

Serving a large roast bird has been a traditional way to mark special occasions, particularly Thanksgiving and Christmas. The increasing popularity of turkey, and its greater availability, mean that you can use it to celebrate events at any time of year.

BABY TURKEY WITH A HERB CRUST

This recipe is particularly recommended for small turkeys, but it is also suitable for roasting chickens. The bird can also be stuffed, in which case the flavor of the stuffing should be coordinated with that of the crust. A stuffing made from the giblets and seasoned with the same herb mixture as the crust is particularly suitable.

Serves 4

one 5½-lb baby turkey
1 teaspoon salt, freshly ground white pepper
6 tablespoons unsalted butter
For the herb crust:
1 cup fresh bread crumbs
¼ cup coarsely ground almonds
4 tablespoons chopped fresh herbs: parsley, sage, and thyme in equal proportions, a little rosemary and lovage

Preheat the oven to 400°F. Carefully wash the turkey inside and out and pat dry with paper towels. Season the skin and the stomach cavity with salt and pepper. Truss the turkey as described on the right, place on a rack in a roasting pan, and put in the oven. After 5 minutes, brush with butter. Mix together all the ingredients for the herb crust. After about 40 minutes, sprinkle all over the turkey. From time to time, spoon the mixture of melted butter and herbs that drips into the roasting pan over the turkey. After a further 30 minutes, pierce the thigh with a skewer to check whether the turkey is cooked; cook longer if necessary. Allow the cooked turkey to rest for about 15 minutes wrapped in foil, then carve and serve.

To truss the turkey:

Pull kitchen string through under the legs. Turn the turkey onto the breast, and cross the string over.

Turn onto the back, take the string between the legs and the breast, cross over on the breast, and tie together at the joints.

During roasting brush the turkey several times with the melted butter, and sprinkle with the herb mixture halfway through the cooking time.

THANKSGIVING TURKEY

Although as individuals we are more than likely to hold differing opinions on many issues, there is one point on which all Americans agree: turkey is definitely the main feature of Thanksgiving Day dinner. For most of us, the feast just would not be complete without the traditional accompaniments of cranberry sauce and corn, but there are innumerable variations on what else to serve with it, as well as different ways to prepare the stuffing and the cranberries. Here, then, are more recipes for this most important meal.

Serves 4–6
one 8-lb turkey
salt, freshly ground white pepper
3 tablespoons vegetable oil
For the stuffing:
5 slices day-old white bread
10 oz apples
1 cup chopped onions
½ cup chopped celery
7 teaspoons unsalted butter
1 cup corn kernels
⅓ cup raisins
⅔ cup chopped walnuts
1 tablespoon chopped fresh herbs: thyme and oregano
salt, freshly ground pepper
1 egg
For the cranberry sauce:
1 lb cranberries
1 cup brown sugar
juice of ½ lemon
¼ cup red wine
¼ teaspoon cinnamon
½ teaspoon mustard powder
¼ teaspoon ground ginger
grated zest and juice of 1 orange
For the corn:
4 ears of corn
salt, 4 leek leaves

Wash the turkey inside and out under cold running water. To make the stuffing, soak the bread in just a little water. Peel the apples, remove the core, and dice the flesh. Melt the butter in a large pan and sweat the onion and celery. Add the corn kernels, apple, raisins, walnuts, and herbs, season with salt and pepper, and stew for 10 minutes. Transfer to a dish and allow to cool. Squeeze the bread out well and mix with the egg. Add to the stuffing and mix together well, and season again. Season the turkey inside with salt and pepper, then stuff. Close the opening with skewers and string. To truss the turkey, tuck in the wings, take the string from underneath around the end of the legs and cross over at the joints. Take the string down the side of the turkey, along the lower legs to the wings and pull tight. Pull the string around and tie it securely at the side.

Preheat the oven to 325°F. Season the outside of the turkey with salt and pepper, and rub with oil. Place it in a roasting pan and roast for at least 3 hours (20 minutes per pound — remember to allow for the additional weight of the stuffing — plus 20 minutes), basting from time to time with the cooking juices, until crispy and brown. At the end of the cooking time, pierce the thigh with a skewer; if the juices run clear, the turkey is fully cooked.

In the meantime, carefully pick over the cranberries, wash, and drain. Cook in a large saucepan with the sugar and lemon juice, stirring constantly, for about 15 minutes. Add the red wine, spices, and orange zest and juice, stir, and cook for a further 10 minutes.

To make the corn, place the ears in a large saucepan of boiling salted water, cover, and cook for 20 minutes. Wash the leek leaves and blanch. Remove the corn from the water and tie the leek leaves around them. Serve the turkey and stuffing with the cranberry sauce and the corn.

BISTILLA, THE SQUAB PIE FROM MOROCCO

Instead of the expensive, paper-thin *warkha* pastry, use phyllo pastry. For the *bistilla*, cut the sheets into round shapes, and for the guinea fowl pie on the opposite page, cut them into rectangles.

Serves 4

4 squabs, with heart and liver
½ teaspoon salt, freshly ground white pepper
1 cup unsalted butter
1¾ cups diced onions
2 tablespoons chopped fresh parsley, 1 teaspoon fresh thyme leaves
2 teaspoons freshly grated ginger
½ teaspoon cumin, 2 pinches turmeric
1 cup water
4 eggs, beaten
1 cup shelled almonds
½ teaspoon cinnamon, 1 tablespoon sugar
20 sheets phyllo pastry
3 tablespoons oil
To sprinkle over:
1 tablespoon confectioners' sugar, ½ teaspoon cinnamon

Wash the squabs inside and out, pat dry, and season with salt and pepper. Finely dice the giblets. Melt half the butter in a pan, sear the squabs on all sides and remove. Brown the onions and the giblets in the butter remaining in the pan. Add the herbs, spices, and the water, and bring to a boil. Add the squabs, cover, and braise for about 50 minutes, then remove, take the meat off the bones and chop finely. Pour off half of the broth and reserve. Reduce the remaining broth over a high heat to about ¼ cup, skim, and reserve. Now heat the reserved broth, thicken with the beaten eggs, and add the reduced stock. Melt ¼ cup of the butter in a frying pan, lightly brown the almonds, drain, chop finely, and mix with the cinnamon and sugar.

Arrange 6 rounds of pastry, each overlapping, into a closed circle, brush with a little melted butter, and place another circle of 6 rounds on top. Spread half the almond mixture in the middle. Mix the squab meat with the sauce, place on the almond mixture and cover with the remaining almond mixture. Fold the edges of the top layer of pastry over the pie filling, cover with the remaining rounds of phyllo, brush with a little melted butter, and fold up the edges of the bottom layer of pastry. Heat the oil and the remaining butter in a large frying pan, slide the pie into the hot fat, fry for about 5 minutes until golden brown, carefully turn with a spatula and the aid of a pan lid, and fry the other side. Slide onto a serving plate, sprinkle with sugar and cinnamon in a lattice pattern, and serve hot.

Handling the phyllo pastry: The success of the pie depends on the correct laying out, filling, and combining of the pastry sheets. To keep them moist so that they do not break when folded, brush each layer with melted butter. Cover spare sheets with a damp cloth until ready to use.

Poultry pies from the pan
Hearty fillings in thin pastry

The origins of these delicacies are not proven, but they are most probably to be found in Arabia. These pies are still prepared today in the countries of North Africa, and Morocco is famous for its *bistillas*, delicious squab pies. Pies are made there, however, not only with squab, but also with chicken and turkey. The most important feature of these pies is their paper-thin pastry, which is known in Morocco as *warkha*. The elastic dough is pressed onto a hot plate and then pulled off. The thin film of pastry that sticks to the plate is then baked. This is a very difficult procedure, and a simple alternative is to use phyllo pastry.

To make the guinea fowl pie:

Preheat the oven to 400°F. Divide the guinea fowl into legs, wings, and breasts. Brown on all sides in the hot oil until crisp, remove and drain.

In the fat that is left, brown the chopped carcass with the giblets, then add the diced onions, and sweat.

Melt the butter in a large frying pan. Slide the pastry into the pan and fry for 5 minutes on each side, or until crisp and brown.

Add the spices, dust with flour, add the chopped carrots and celeriac, and pour on the chicken stock.

Return the pieces of guinea fowl to the pan and roast for approximately 40 minutes. Remove, take off the meat, and chop finely.

Strain the cooking liquid, then reduce by about three quarters and add the guinea fowl meat.

Add the herbs and eggs to the mixture, mix everything together well and, if necessary, adjust the seasoning.

GUINEA FOWL PIE

Serves 8–10 as an appetizer

one 4½-lb guinea fowl, with giblets

¼ cup vegetable oil, 1¼ cups diced onions

1 teaspoon salt, freshly ground white pepper

1 chile pepper, seeded

1 teaspoon freshly grated ginger

½ teaspoon turmeric, 2 lightly crushed garlic cloves

1 tablespoon flour

⅓ cup each chopped carrots and celeriac

3¼ cups light poultry stock (see pages 52–3)

2 tablespoons chopped fresh herbs: cilantro, parsley, and thyme

4 hard-boiled eggs

10 sheets phyllo pastry

½ cup coarsely ground almonds, ½ teaspoon cinnamon, 6 tablespoons unsalted butter

Make the guinea fowl pie as described in the picture sequence to the right.

Overlap the pastry sheets to form a large rectangle. Spread the almonds mixed with the cinnamon in the center and place the meat on top.

Fold the 4 sides of the pastry sheets over the filling, so that it is completely enclosed and nothing runs out.

Barbecuing

Barbecuing is an ideal method for cooking poultry, as whole birds and individual cuts can be prepared in the optimum way to suit their natural characteristics. It is also a simple and extremely efficient method of preparing a meal: potatoes, corn on the cob, onions, and even zucchini can cook in the coals while the meat cooks on top.

Marinating the meat before cooking, and stuffing whole birds under the skin are ways to enhance the natural flavor of the meat, and they provide welcome alternatives to the familiar tomato-based barbecue sauce. To get the ultimate benefit of a marinade, leave the poultry to steep in it in the refrigerator overnight. Take the meat out of the refrigerator some time before you want to cook it to allow it to return to room temperature.

Wrapping portions of meat in bacon before grilling adds flavor
and ensures that the meat does not dry out.

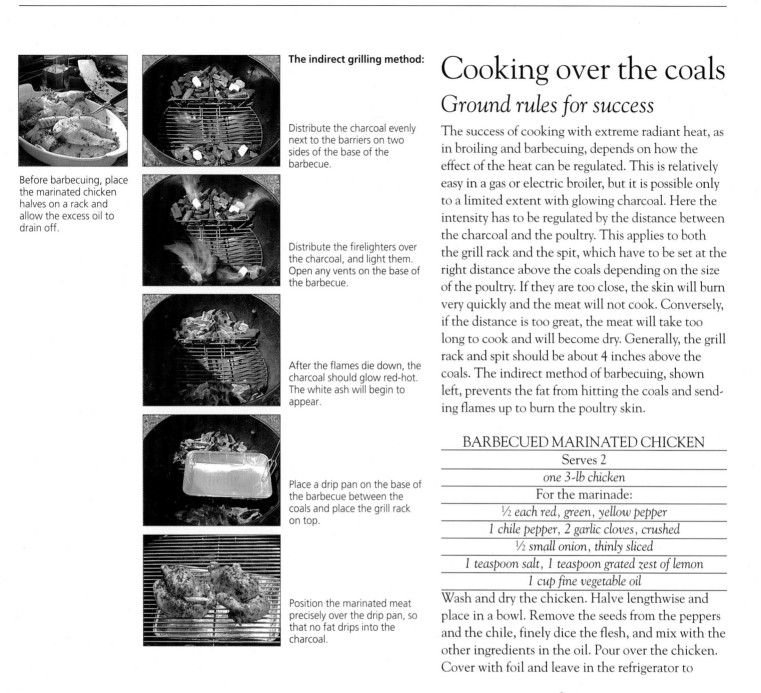

Before barbecuing, place the marinated chicken halves on a rack and allow the excess oil to drain off.

The indirect grilling method:

Distribute the charcoal evenly next to the barriers on two sides of the base of the barbecue.

Distribute the firelighters over the charcoal, and light them. Open any vents on the base of the barbecue.

After the flames die down, the charcoal should glow red-hot. The white ash will begin to appear.

Place a drip pan on the base of the barbecue between the coals and place the grill rack on top.

Position the marinated meat precisely over the drip pan, so that no fat drips into the charcoal.

Cooking over the coals
Ground rules for success

The success of cooking with extreme radiant heat, as in broiling and barbecuing, depends on how the effect of the heat can be regulated. This is relatively easy in a gas or electric broiler, but it is possible only to a limited extent with glowing charcoal. Here the intensity has to be regulated by the distance between the charcoal and the poultry. This applies to both the grill rack and the spit, which have to be set at the right distance above the coals depending on the size of the poultry. If they are too close, the skin will burn very quickly and the meat will not cook. Conversely, if the distance is too great, the meat will take too long to cook and will become dry. Generally, the grill rack and spit should be about 4 inches above the coals. The indirect method of barbecuing, shown left, prevents the fat from hitting the coals and sending flames up to burn the poultry skin.

BARBECUED MARINATED CHICKEN

Serves 2
one 3-lb chicken
For the marinade:
½ each red, green, yellow pepper
1 chile pepper, 2 garlic cloves, crushed
½ small onion, thinly sliced
1 teaspoon salt, 1 teaspoon grated zest of lemon
1 cup fine vegetable oil

Wash and dry the chicken. Halve lengthwise and place in a bowl. Remove the seeds from the peppers and the chile, finely dice the flesh, and mix with the other ingredients in the oil. Pour over the chicken. Cover with foil and leave in the refrigerator to

A well-seasoned barbecued chicken can be accompanied by simple things, such as fresh French bread or crisp fried potatoes.

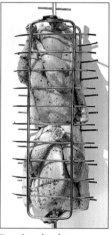

Two in a basket: a neat way to barbecue tiny squabs.

marinate overnight. Grill on both sides for a total of 40 minutes. Baste frequently with the marinade while cooking.

CHICKEN MARTINIQUE

In this recipe the delicate flavor of the chicken combines superbly with the devilish heat of the chiles. The result is a chicken with delicious, juicy flesh, and a spicy, crisp crust. Caribbean chiles have a powerful but very flavorful heat, but other hot varieties can also be used. However, there is no substitute for the limes. Their typical flavor cannot be replaced, for example, by lemons.

Serves 2
one 3-lb chicken
For the marinade:
finely grated rind and juice of 1 lime
1 garlic clove, crushed
1 teaspoon salt
1½ tablespoons chopped fresh ginger
freshly grated nutmeg
2 tablespoons freshly chopped herbs: parsley, cilantro, thyme, and basil
¼ cup fine vegetable oil
1 chile pepper

Wash the chicken inside and out, and carefully pat dry. Divide along the backbone with a heavy knife or poultry shears. Place the two halves with the cut side uppermost in a large shallow dish. Place the lime rind and juice in a cup. Add the garlic, salt, ginger, nutmeg, and half of the chopped herbs. Pour in the oil and mix well. First drizzle the mixture over the cut surfaces of the chicken halves, then turn them over and pour the remainder of the marinade over the other side. Halve the chile pepper lengthwise, seed, cut the flesh into strips, and scatter over the chicken. Cover with foil and leave in the refrigerator to marinate overnight.

Remove the majority of the chile strips, brush the chicken halves well with the marinade that has drained off, and place on the grill. First grill on the cut side for 10 minutes, then turn and cook on the skin side for a further 15–20 minutes, until the skin is crisp and the meat is cooked.

Traditionally, Chicken Martinique is served with breadfruit and rice, but, of course, you can serve it with other vegetables too. The typical condiment on the table is a chile pepper halved lengthwise, with the seeds removed, and freshly squeezed lime juice poured into the halves. The chile half is then squeezed over the chicken in order to sprinkle it with the flavor of the lime juice and the heat of the chile.

Kebabs

An endless spectrum of colorful surprises

The variety of ingredients that can be used to make kebabs is almost unlimited. Poultry can be combined with a wide range of other food, such as shellfish, vegetables, and fruit. In order to protect lean meat from drying out, wrap it in bacon. Then you need to brush only a little fat onto the kebabs to prevent them from sticking to the grill. Naturally, the salty bacon also imparts flavor to the meat. If you prefer not to use bacon, coat the kebabs well with fat and make sure they cook quickly. It is important that the kebabs are not directly over the charcoal, as fat that drips down onto it encourages the formation of carcinogens. Depending on the heat of the embers, allow 8–12 minutes cooking time. When grilled properly, colorful kebabs are a welcome change for a barbecue party.

CHICKEN WITH GIANT SHRIMP

Makes 2 kebabs

6 oz chicken breast

4 giant shrimp, heads removed

4–6 cocktail onions

salt, freshly ground white pepper, lemon juice

Cut the chicken breast with the skin into large pieces and place on skewers, alternating with the shrimp and onions. Season with salt and pepper, and grill. Before serving, sprinkle some drops of lemon juice on the kebabs.

TURKEY WITH MUSHROOMS

Makes 2 kebabs

½ lb turkey scallop, about ½-inch thick

4 button mushrooms

2 cèpe mushrooms

2 slices bacon

2 wedges of apple

½ small onion

salt, freshly ground white pepper

chopped fresh herbs

Cut the turkey scallop into 4 equal pieces. Clean the button mushrooms. Clean the cèpe mushrooms and wrap each one in a slice of bacon. Halve the onion half and the apple wedges, and place on skewers alternating with the turkey pieces, button mushrooms, and cèpe mushrooms, as shown left, and season with salt and pepper. After grilling, sprinkle with chopped fresh herbs of your choice.

DUCK AND PEPPER KEBAB

Makes 2 kebabs

6 oz duck breast

½ each red and yellow pepper

4 garlic cloves, unpeeled

herbes de Provence (optional)

salt, freshly ground white pepper

Roughly dice the duck breast. Remove the seeds and stalk from the peppers, and cut the flesh into chunks. Lightly press the garlic with the ball of the hand, so that the peel comes away slightly.

Alternate the ingredients on the skewer, and arrange the duck so that the skin is all facing one direction. Season the kebabs with salt and pepper, and grill for slightly longer on the skin side, so that it is pleasantly crisp. Sprinkle with *herbes de Provence* if desired.

SQUAB AND SAGE KEBABS

Makes 2 kebabs

two ¾-lb squabs

6 fresh sage leaves

salt, freshly ground white pepper

For the sauce:

2 tablespoons unsalted butter

2 shallots, finely chopped

1½ tablespoons cognac

½ cup dark poultry stock (see pages 50–1)

Wash the squabs, pat dry, divide into breasts and legs, and arrange on the skewers alternating with the sage leaves. Before grilling, make the sauce from the carcasses. Finely chop the bones, brown in 2 teaspoons of butter, add the shallots, and sweat. Chill the remaining butter. Pour on the cognac, ignite and flambé the carcasses. Pour on the poultry stock, reduce to about half, and strain. Season and grill the kebabs. Shortly before the end of the cooking time, cut the remaining butter into cubes and whisk into the hot sauce, adjust the seasoning, and serve with the kebabs.

Grilled on the spit
The ideal way to barbecue a whole bird

The spit can be used for all types of poultry, from squab to turkey. When the meat is rotated evenly, the effect of the heat on all parts is uniform. To ensure a crisp skin and juicy meat, set the spit at the correct distance from the coals, and brush the poultry frequently with the dripping, so that the surface cannot dry out. For lean poultry, use a mixture of ⅓ oil and ⅔ butter.

Smaller birds are best cooked in a grilling basket, medium-sized birds on the spit. The maximum size of bird you can barbecue whole is determined by the capacity of the barbecue.

To barbecue the duck:

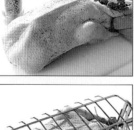

Season the inside and outside of the washed and dried duck with salt and pepper, and place the bouquet garni in the stomach cavity.

Place in a grilling basket or skewer onto a spit and hold in place with the clamps. Put over the hot coals.

Brush frequently with the oil–butter mixture. About 15 minutes before the end of the cooking time, sprinkle on the herbs.

BARBECUED DUCK

Nantais ducks are particularly suitable for grilling because of their low weight and strong flavor, but other types of duck can be substituted.

Serves 2–3

one 3-lb duck
salt, freshly ground white pepper
1 bouquet garni: parsley, sage, and thyme
2 tablespoons vegetable oil
3 tablespoons unsalted butter
2 teaspoons hot paprika
2 tablespoons chopped fresh herbs (parsley, sage, thyme)

Prepare and grill the duck as shown in the picture sequence to the left. The cooking time is 60–70 minutes.

Serve with potatoes cooked in the coals and a light mixed salad.

After roasting, let the duck rest for about 10 minutes before carving, to give the juices time to be redistributed.

To stuff young guinea fowl under the skin:

Process the washed herbs with the toast, and season with salt and pepper. Add the pine nuts and chop finely.

Using a pair of poultry shears, cut the guinea fowls open along the backbone, clean the stomach cavity, and season with salt and pepper.

Place the guinea fowls on a chopping board with the breast side uppermost and press flat lightly with the ball of the hand.

Starting from the neck, loosen the skin from the breast meat with your fingers, being careful not to tear it.

Carefully push the stuffing under the skin with a spoon, and spread it evenly over the meat.

Press lightly with the fingers to give shape to the stuffing. Make an incision about ¾-inch long in the thin skin between the legs.

Carefully pull the legs through the slit in order to maintain the shape of the bird during cooking.

Serve the guinea fowl with grilled slices of zucchini and eggplant, and pieces of cooked tomato.

YOUNG GUINEA FOWL STUFFED UNDER THE SKIN

This recipe is for a small guinea fowl cooked on a spit or in a grilling basket (see opposite page). If it is to be cooked on the grill itself, cut it open and press it flat, so that it cooks quickly and evenly.

Serves 2

two 1-lb young guinea fowls
salt, freshly ground white pepper
For the stuffing:
1 small bunch fresh flat-leaf parsley
2 sprigs each fresh thyme and rosemary
1 slice toast, finely chopped
salt, freshly ground white pepper
2½ tablespoons pine nuts

Make the stuffing as shown in the first picture in the sequence to the right. Follow the instructions accompanying the subsequent pictures to clean and prepare the guinea fowls. Stuff them carefully, as shown.

If you are not cooking the birds on the spit, grill them on their backs for the first 20 minutes, then turn them over and grill for a further 15–20 minutes, remembering to baste them from time to time so that the meat does not dry out.

Whichever method you use, there should still be sufficient space on the grill to cook slices of vegetables to accompany the guinea fowl. Alternatively, you may like to try wrapping whole zucchini in foil and cooking them in the coals.

Baking and deep-frying

Poultry cooked in the oven does not always have to be roasted; it is also excellent baked. Inside a protective casing of salt, for example, the characteristic taste of poultry becomes concentrated, and the result is juicy meat that does not taste at all salty. Whether encrusted in salt or in bread dough, or used to fill spicy tartlets or a quiche, versatile poultry meat proves to be a true delicacy. Smoked turkey and chicken add a fine flavor to a pizza; smoked duck breast makes it a real treat.

Gourmets may argue about the virtues of deep-frying, but you will get excellent results if you coat the meat correctly and fry it at the right temperature.

A delicacy in bread dough: a seared breast of chicken with veal and herb stuffing.

Deep-fried poultry

A crispy coating of flour, egg, and bread crumbs keeps the meat juicy

When protected by a coating of bread crumbs, all types of poultry — provided they are not too large — can be fried in hot fat. The coating forms a hermetic seal; the surface becomes crisp, while the inside remains juicy. Usually, the meat is rolled in flour, dipped into beaten egg, and coated in bread crumbs. The flavor can be varied by adding almonds or Parmesan cheese. Be careful that the coating covers all of the meat; if necessary, repeat the procedure. The amount of oil used is also important: the pieces should "swim" in it, so that the heat can penetrate evenly. Use a deep pot and do not fill it more than halfway. Always use small pieces of meat so that the surface does not become too brown before the inside is hot.

FRIED CHICKEN

The oil should be 365°F. If you do not have a frying thermometer, drop a small cube of bread into the fat; if it browns in 1 minute, the oil is the right temperature.

Serves 4
one 2-lb chicken
½ teaspoon salt
freshly ground white pepper
2 tablespoons all-purpose flour
2 eggs, beaten
1 cup dried bread crumbs
vegetable oil for frying

Wash the chicken and pat dry. Divide into 4 or 8 pieces as desired and again dry carefully with paper towels, so that the coating adheres well. Season with salt and pepper, and coat as described in the picture sequence below, pressing the bread crumbs well into place. Deep-fry for 12–15 minutes, then test with a skewer to check that it is thoroughly cooked.

TURKEY ROLLS

The piquant filling of prosciutto and Fontina cheese makes the turkey really spicy. Under the protective crust of eggs and bread crumbs, the meat remains pleasantly juicy.

Serves 4
8 thin slices of turkey breast, about 2 oz each
½ garlic clove
1 teaspoon strong mustard, ½ teaspoon salt
8 thin slices prosciutto
8 thin slices Fontina cheese
2 tablespoons all-purpose flour
2 eggs
⅔ cup dried bread crumbs

Beat the turkey scallops evenly. Finely crush the garlic, mix with the mustard and the salt, and brush a thin coating of this onto the scallops. Cover with ham and cheese as shown below, roll up, and secure with a toothpick. Carefully coat with bread crumbs and deep-fry for 10–12 minutes until crisp.

First turn the carefully dried, seasoned chicken pieces in the flour, then in the egg, making sure that it coats them completely. Carefully roll the pieces in the bread crumbs, pressing firmly into place, then tap them lightly to remove any excess. Deep-fry in hot oil.

Place 1 slice each of ham and cheese on the prepared turkey scallops, roll up and secure with a toothpick. Dip the rolls in flour, tapping off the excess, then roll them in the beaten eggs and then in the bread crumbs, pressing the crumbs firmly into place. Deep-fry in the hot oil.

Baked in a crust of salt

This cooking method suits lean poultry best, but it can also be used for ducklings from which the abdominal fat has been removed. The salt crust seals the meat so that during cooking the fat cannot run out. You will not need to salt the cooked meat, but it will not be too salty either.

CHICKEN IN A SALT CRUST

The salt crust is bound with egg white, and the meat cooks gently in its own juice. The bird can be encased in the salt crust directly on a baking sheet lined with foil, but it is simpler to place the bird in a large oval casserole lined with a layer of salt and to pile the salt paste up around it, as shown here.

Serves 4
one 4-lb chicken
2 garlic cloves, unpeeled
freshly ground white pepper
1 bouquet garni: parsley, sage, thyme, and lovage
For the salt paste:
11 lb coarse salt, 1 egg white, water

Wash the chicken and carefully pat dry. Crush the garlic cloves with the back of a knife. Season the stomach cavity with pepper, and insert the bouquet garni and the garlic cloves. Mix the salt with the egg white and sufficient water into a pliable paste. Preheat the oven to 425°F. Line a casserole with a ¾-inch thick layer of salt paste, place the chicken on it, and pile the remaining salt paste up around it, so that the chicken is completely sealed in. Place on the lowest rack of the oven and cook for about 2 hours. Break open the salt casing with a hammer or a meat mallet and remove the chicken. Serve with salad and freshly baked white bread.

ONION TARTLETS
WITH SMOKED LEG OF TURKEY

Makes eight 4-inch tartlets

For the pastry:

2½ cups all-purpose flour, ¾ cup unsalted butter

salt, 3–4 tablespoons water, 1 egg

For the filling:

3 tablespoons unsalted butter

2–3 slices smoked bacon, finely chopped

1¼ cup diced onion

2 sliced leek

1 clove, finely crushed garlic

½ cup light poultry stock (see pages 52–3)

8 oz smoked turkey thigh

½ cup light cream, 2 eggs

1 cup shredded Emmenthal cheese

salt, freshly ground white pepper

To make the pastry:
Rub the flour and butter by hand until it has the consistency of bread crumbs. Make a well in the middle, add salt, water and the egg, and knead quickly into a smooth dough. Chill for 1 hour, roll out, and line the pans with the aid of a rolling pin.

To make the onion tartlets: Bake the pastry blind, as described in the recipe. Allow to cool, remove the baking beans and parchment. Fill with the meat, top with the onion mixture, and bake.

Make the pastry as described to the left. Roll it out to ⅛-inch thick, line the greased tartlet tins with it and cut off the overhanging edges. Bake the pastry blind: prick the base of the pastry all over with a fork, line it with baking parchment, weigh down with baking beans, and bake for 10 minutes at 400°F. This prevents the base from softening when filled later.

To make the filling, melt half the butter in a pan, add the smoked bacon, and fry until brown but not crisp. Add the onion, the leek, and the garlic, and stew for about 5 minutes. Add the stock and continue to cook until the liquid has evaporated. Set the mixture aside. Preheat the oven to 415°F. Dice the turkey meat. Melt the remaining butter in a clean pan and briefly sear the turkey. Mix the cream, eggs, and cheese into the onion mixture, season with salt and pepper, and proceed as described to the left. Bake the filled tartlets for 25–30 minutes until golden brown. Serve hot.

OLIVE AND CHICKEN QUICHE

Serves 4

1 recipe pastry (see left)

For the filling:

8 oz chicken breast

¼ cup unsalted butter

¾ cup diced onion, 1 garlic clove

½ cup chopped zucchini

⅓ cup each yellow, red, and green pepper

1 cup diced chicken liver

2 tablespoons chopped fresh herbs: parsley, thyme, and oregano

12 large black olives

For the topping:

1½ cups light cream, 3 eggs

1 teaspoon salt, freshly ground black pepper

¼ teaspoon each grated nutmeg and mace

Line a greased 10-inch quiche dish with the rolled out pastry, press down at the edges, and cut off the overhanging pastry. Prick the base of the pastry all over with a fork, line it with baking parchment, weigh down with baking beans, and bake for 10 minutes at 400°F. Finely dice the chicken. Melt 2 tablespoons of butter in a frying pan, fry the meat for 4–5 minutes, remove, and set aside. Melt the rest of the butter, and sweat the onion and garlic. Add the zucchini and peppers, and continue to sweat for about 5 minutes. Add the chicken liver. Finally, mix in the herbs and allow to cool a little. Mix the cream with the eggs and spices. Mix the meat with the vegetable mixture and fill the pastry. Scatter the olives evenly on the quiche. Pour in the egg and cream mixture, and bake in the oven for 45–50 minutes until golden brown.

Crisp-baked dough as a base and casing

For browned surfaces or delicate fillings

Whether for a tartlet, a quiche, large spicy cakes, a pie or a pastry casing, a crisp-baked dough makes it possible to vary the dish and add flavor. Its appeal lies in the crust, the taste of which is so subtle that it does not mask the other gentle flavors .

GOOSE LIVER IN BRIOCHE DOUGH

This combination is unsurpassed: the *foie gras* develops particularly well in this casing and the brioche dough benefits from the flavor of the liver.

For a bread pan about 12 x 5 x 3 inches
one 1¾-lb goose liver
½ teaspoon salt
pinch each of ground allspice and nutmeg
freshly ground white pepper
1 cup vintage port
1½ tablespoons Armagnac
For the brioche dough:
2 tablespoons dry yeast, ½ cup lukewarm milk
¾ cup unsalted butter
2 eggs, ½ teaspoon sugar
1 teaspoon salt
1 lb all-purpose flour
Also:
4 thin slices of bacon fat
1–2 egg yolks

Carefully remove all skin and veins from the liver, season with salt, place in a dish and pour on the port and Armagnac. Cover with foil, place in the refrigerator, and marinate for 24 hours. Remove the liver from the marinade and drain. Boil the marinade and reduce to about 2–3 tablespoons, then cool. Press half of the liver into a bread pan somewhat smaller than the final pan, pour the reduced marinade over it, and add the remaining liver. To make the dough, dissolve the yeast in the lukewarm milk, stirring all the time. Melt the butter, allow to cool, and add the eggs, sugar, and salt. Sift the flour into a bowl, add the dissolved yeast and the butter mixture, and knead into a smooth, dry dough. Cover the dough with a cloth, and leave to rise at room temperature for 30 minutes. Roll out to 16 x 24 inches, and use it to line a second, somewhat larger bread pan so that the dough overhangs about 2½ inches on all sides. Turn out the liver prepared earlier, wrap it in the thin slices of bacon fat, and place it in the pan lined with dough. Brush the overhanging edges of the dough with egg yolk, fold together over the filling, and press together well so that the liver is completely enclosed. Using a sharp knife, cut two small crosses into the surface, insert two small pie vents to act as chimneys, and surround them with rosettes of dough. Allow the pie to rise at room temperature, no warmer, for 20–30 minutes, until its volume has almost doubled. Preheat the oven to 415°F. Brush the surface of the loaf with egg yolk and bake for 45–55 minutes. Cool overnight. Remove the vents.

Pizzas large and small
Smoked poultry adds a special flavor

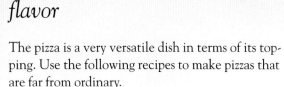

The pizza is a very versatile dish in terms of its topping. Use the following recipes to make pizzas that are far from ordinary.

BASIC RECIPE FOR PIZZA DOUGH

Makes two 12-inch pizzas
2½ cups all-purpose flour, 2 tablespoons yeast
½ cup lukewarm water
½ teaspoon salt, 2 tablespoons olive oil

This quite simple yeast dough recipe contains no eggs, butter, or milk — only water — which makes the pizza base nice and crispy when baked. The dough should be firm yet elastic, so that it can be well stretched without tearing. The edge must always be thicker than the rest of the pizza base so that the liquid in the topping does not run into the oven during baking.

To make the pizza dough: Make a well in the flour, add the lukewarm water and dissolve the yeast in it. Cover with flour, cover the bowl with a cloth, and leave in a warm place to rise until the surface cracks. Add the oil and mix in.

On a floured working surface, knead to a smooth dough. Allow to rise again to double the volume.

Cut the dough into pieces, roll them into balls, and then roll out into bases with a rolling pin.

With floured hands, stroke the bases from the center outwards. Prick several times with a fork.

Top the bases with the ingredients in the correct sequence, but leave a space at the slightly raised edge.

SMOKED CHICKEN PIZZA

The piquancy of this pizza comes from the smoked chicken. As an alternative, try smoked turkey, preferably using meat from the thigh, as the breast meat is too dry.

Makes two 12-inch pizzas
1 recipe basic pizza dough
For the topping:
10 oz tomatoes
6 scallions without tips
1 each red, yellow, and green pepper
2 small zucchini
½ boned smoked chicken, about 1½ lb
½ teaspoon salt, pepper
10 oz mozzarella cheese
16 black olives
2 tablespoons chopped fresh thyme, oregano, and basil
¼ cup fine olive oil

Preheat the oven to 425°F. Slice the tomatoes and distribute over the dough bases. Finely chop the scallion and sprinkle on top of the tomatoes. Core and seed the peppers, and cut into fine strips. Slice the zucchini and the mozzarella. Cut the meat into slices and distribute on the pizza with strips of pepper and the zucchini. Season with salt and pepper, and top with the mozzarella. Add the olives, sprinkle with the herbs, and drizzle with oil. Bake for around 25 minutes until the edge of the dough is crispy and brown.

Add the diced tomatoes to the sweated onions. Stew, then add the tomato paste.

MINI-PIZZAS WITH SMOKED DUCK BREAST

These delicate morsels are ideal as canapés, snacks, or appetizers. The duck breast combined with the homemade tomato sauce produces a quite special topping.

Makes 12 mini-pizzas
1 recipe basic pizza dough
For the tomato sauce:
2 tablespoons fine olive oil, ½ cup diced onion
1 garlic clove, finely chopped
½ lb tomatoes, 1 tablespoon tomato paste
½ teaspoon salt, freshly ground pepper
2 tablespoons chopped fresh herbs: for example, parsley, basil, rosemary, thyme
For the topping:
1 tablespoon unsalted butter
2½ cups sliced fresh mushrooms, 1 yellow pepper
14 oz sliced smoked duck breast
6 oz mozzarella cheese, chopped
2 tablespoons chopped chives, ¼ cup olive oil

Preheat the oven to 425°F. Divide the dough into 12 equal-sized balls. Allow the dough to rise a little again, then roll out into bases with a diameter of 4 inches, and place on two baking sheets.

To make the sauce, heat the oil, sweat the onions, add the garlic, and cook lightly. Dice and add the tomatoes, and stew for 10 minutes until soft. Add the tomato paste, salt, pepper, and mixed herbs, and stew for a further 5 minutes. In another pan, heat the butter and sweat the mushrooms. Dice the pepper and add to the pan. Spread tomato sauce on the pizza bases, then distribute the duck, the vegetable mixture, and the cheese. Sprinkle with chives, drizzle with oil, and bake for 30 minutes.

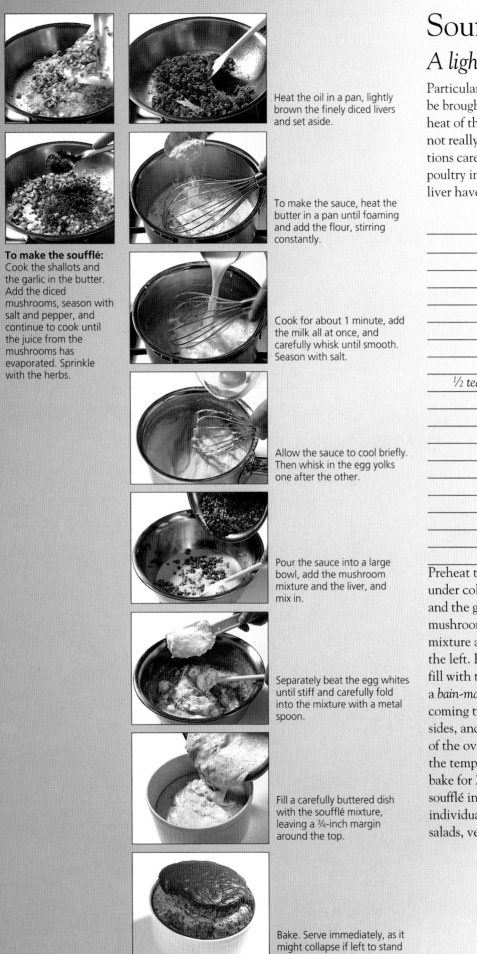

Heat the oil in a pan, lightly brown the finely diced livers and set aside.

To make the soufflé:
Cook the shallots and the garlic in the butter. Add the diced mushrooms, season with salt and pepper, and continue to cook until the juice from the mushrooms has evaporated. Sprinkle with the herbs.

To make the sauce, heat the butter in a pan until foaming and add the flour, stirring constantly.

Cook for about 1 minute, add the milk all at once, and carefully whisk until smooth. Season with salt.

Allow the sauce to cool briefly. Then whisk in the egg yolks one after the other.

Pour the sauce into a large bowl, add the mushroom mixture and the liver, and mix in.

Separately beat the egg whites until stiff and carefully fold into the mixture with a metal spoon.

Fill a carefully buttered dish with the soufflé mixture, leaving a ¾-inch margin around the top.

Bake. Serve immediately, as it might collapse if left to stand for too long.

Soufflés and puddings
A light way with liver

Particularly airy soufflés are very sensitive and must be brought to the table as soon as they have left the heat of the oven, as they collapse easily. They are not really difficult to make if you follow the directions carefully. You can use the livers of any type of poultry in a soufflé, although those made with duck liver have a particularly strong flavor.

POULTRY LIVER SOUFFLÉ
Serves 4–6
7 oz poultry liver
2 shallots
½ garlic clove
¼ lb button mushrooms
1½ tablespoons unsalted butter
salt, freshly ground white pepper
1 tablespoon chopped fresh parsley
½ teaspoon chopped fresh thyme and rosemary
2 tablespoons vegetable oil
For the sauce:
7 teaspoons unsalted butter
1½ tablespoons all-purpose flour
1 cup milk
pinch of salt
4 egg yolks
Also:
4 egg whites
butter for the dish

Preheat the oven to 350°F. Rinse the poultry livers under cold water, pat dry, and dice. Peel the shallots and the garlic, and chop finely. Wash and peel the mushrooms, and chop finely. Complete the soufflé mixture as shown in the picture sequence to the left. Butter a 2-quart soufflé dish and fill with the mixture. Place the dish in a *bain-marie* with hot water (175°F) coming two-thirds of the way up its sides, and bake on the bottom rack of the oven 15 minutes. Increase the temperature to 400°F and bake for 25–30 minutes. Serve the soufflé in the dish, or spoon out individual portions. Serve with salads, vegetables, or sauces.

1 tablespoon chopped fresh parsley

3–4 tablespoons crème fraîche

2 egg whites

Preheat the oven to 350°F. Wash the poultry liver thoroughly under running water, clean, and dice finely. Peel the shallot and dice finely. Melt 2½ teaspoons of butter in a frying pan, brown the shallot and liver, season with salt and pepper, and transfer to a bowl. After removing the crusts, dice the toast, fry in 2 teaspoons of butter until golden brown, add to the liver, and allow to cool a little. In the meantime, peel and core the apple, dice finely, and marinate in the Calvados and sugar syrup before adding it to the liver. Stir in the egg yolks, parsley, and crème fraîche. Beat the egg whites until stiff and fold in. Fill 4 buttered ramekins with the mixture. Place in a bain-marie (see right) and place a quarter of the remaining butter on each. Place on the bottom rack of the oven and bake for 30–35 minutes. Turn out the ramekins and arrange. A vegetable ragout, such as the one here made from asparagus, is a very suitable accompaniment.

A **bain-marie** is a pan of hot water, about 176°F, which comes about two-thirds of the way up the sides of the filled soufflé dish or ramekins. The *bain-marie* should not boil, nor should it cool to below 176°F.

POULTRY LIVER PUDDING WITH APPLES

Puddings are the more robust cousins of soufflés. But they, too, are light and remain juicy, especially when they are made with apples, as in this recipe.

Serves 4

7 oz poultry liver
1 shallot
7 teaspoons unsalted butter
salt
freshly ground white pepper
3 slices toast
1 tart apple
2 teaspoons Calvados
2 tablespoons sugar syrup
2 egg yolks

Far Eastern specialties

In the national cuisines of Asian countries poultry is handled particularly well, part of a tradition stretching back over many centuries. The most popular poultry that we use in our cooking today — the chicken — is descended from the red jungle chicken, which was indigenous to Southeast Asia and was being kept as domestic poultry as early as 2500 BC. Therefore it is not surprising that, together with duck, it clearly dominates the Asian meat menu.

It is first and foremost the Chinese cooks who, over the millennia, have developed poultry cooking that can justly be described as perfect: you only have to think of the breast and crispy skin of a Peking duck, a delicacy when served with paper-thin rice pancakes and black bean or plum sauce. The true art of Chinese poultry cuisine, however, is really seen when the cooks conjure up the finest dishes from those parts of the duck or chicken that we consider more or less as waste. There are crispy baked chicken wings, braised duck's gizzards, and fine soups made with chicken or duck feet in a spicy mustard sauce. Equally creative use of poultry, in particular chicken, is made by the peoples of Southeast Asia, whose fascinating combinations of spices, fruit, and vegetables of the tropical regions now enrich the international menu.

Eating with chopsticks — this method has strongly influenced the national cuisines of Asia.

There is a wide choice in Asian markets. Whole poultry, pieces of poultry, and giblets are arranged in a clean and appetizing way. Even the feet — which we consider to be waste — are highly sought after, for in China people use them to make an excellent broth. The chickens with the "blue" skin occupy a special place in the range and are always more expensive.

In many Asian countries, where not everyone has a refrigerator, live poultry is sold in the markets. Consumers can see that the birds are in good condition, and are guaranteed freshness.

The Chinese are true artists in the preparation of poultry. The culinary range stretches from the very simple stir-fried chicken with fresh vegetables, as sold in the cookshops on the street, to specialties such as "duck of eight delicacies," which, in terms of the ingredients and the work involved, really can be described as costly.

Chickens, ducks, and the wok

Poultry is the most important meat in the cuisines of Asia, and the wok is used for many different cooking methods

It is true that in the cuisines of Asia, including that of China, not all food is cooked in the wok: there are earthenware pots for soups, and bamboo baskets with matching pots for steaming. Nonetheless, the wok is the universal cooking utensil, a jack-of-all-trades, for it can be used to cook soups, to steam, to deep-fry, and, above all, to stir-fry. In its traditional form (and that is the best), it has a rounded base, is made of cast iron, and has two lateral handles. With an internal diameter of between 10 and 16 inches, it can cope with almost all dishes, except a large whole duck.

For stir-frying, a mainstay of Asian cooking that has become increasingly popular in the West, the wok is almost irreplaceable, particularly for the many delicate poultry dishes. Because table knives are not used in Asia and eating is done primarily with chopsticks, ingredients must be cut into small pieces, which also explains this method of cooking. The meat and the vegetables are cut into bite-sized dice or strips. The empty wok is heated vigorously, then very little oil is added and is evenly distributed by swirling it around inside the wok. The prepared ingredients are added one after the other, in a sequence determined by their required cooking time, and are cooked in an astonishingly short time over a high heat while being stirred constantly. A flat metal utensil with a rounded front, its shape adapted to the wok, is used for stirring. The result of stir-frying is meat that is perfectly cooked — which is especially important in the case of tender poultry — and crunchy fried vegetables with a lot of flavor.

Chicken curries

In Southeast Asia chicken is a favorite ingredient in curries

Spice pastes are traditionally prepared in a mortar, but puréeing in a food processor also produces a very good result.

Curries, which could also be called ragouts with a great deal of sauce, are made with wholly different ingredients depending on their country of origin. The range stretches from quite hot curries with few vegetables and little sauce to soupy, sweet and mild curries. Versatile chicken meat tolerates all seasonings. The delicate flavor of chicken is, it is true, somewhat overwhelmed by hot spices, but can still be tasted. To decrease the heat of a curry, do not use the seeds or membrane of the chile. (Do not get the juice of the chile on your skin, and always wash your hands and any implements immediately after working with chiles.) Curries are served with seasonal vegetables and, of course, rice.

KYETHA HIN

This chicken curry from Burma is made mild by the addition of tomatoes and pumpkin, and the very sparing use of chiles.

Serves 4

| one 3¾-lb fresh roasting chicken |
| 1 onion |
| 2 garlic cloves |
| 1 teaspoon salt |
| ½ teaspoon crushed cardamom |
| 1 tablespoon freshly grated ginger |
| 2 small chile peppers |
| 1 teaspoon turmeric |
| 1 stem lemon grass |
| ¼ cup vegetable oil |
| 2¼ cups light chicken stock (see pages 52–3) |
| 2 large tomatoes |
| ¾–1 cup canned pumpkin chunks |
| 2 teaspoons chopped cilantro |

Cut up the chicken (see pages 24–5) and then cut the meat into bite-sized pieces. Chop the onion and the garlic, and purée finely with the spices and a little oil in a food processor. Heat the remaining oil in the wok, add the purée, and sweat for 2–3 minutes, stirring constantly. Pour in the chicken stock, add the meat, and cook for about 20 minutes over a low heat, stirring constantly. Dice the tomatoes and the pumpkin, add, and simmer everything together over a low heat for a further 30 minutes. Sprinkle with cilantro and serve hot.

CHICKEN CURRY WITH BANANAS

Kukul mas curry is what the Sri Lankans call their outstanding curry, which is certainly devilishly hot. If desired, reduce the spicy heat by removing the seeds from the chile peppers (and remember to wash your hands immediately afterwards). If the curry is still too hot, sprinkle shredded coconut on it.

Curry leaves are a quite typical spice in Sri Lankan curries, but are usually found only in dried form in specialist Asian shops. Unfortunately, when dried, they lose some of their spiciness, which is what gives this dish its unmistakable flavor. However, even without curry leaves, this is a fine, exotic dish, for which bananas provide an interesting complement.

Serves 4
one 3–3½-lb chicken
1 teaspoon salt
1 teaspoon sweet paprika
2 garlic cloves, finely crushed
3 tablespoons vegetable oil
2 tablespoons clarified butter
1 onion, finely chopped
2 teaspoons freshly grated ginger
1 teaspoon turmeric
1 teaspoon chile powder
2 teaspoons ground coriander
1 teaspoon cumin
1 sprig curry leaves (8 fresh or 4 dried)
2¼ cups light chicken stock (see pages 52–3)
3 large bananas
2 red chiles, seeded and cut in rings
freshly shredded coconut (optional)

Cut the chicken into 12–16 pieces of equal size, place in a bowl, sprinkle with salt, paprika, and garlic, and drizzle with the vegetable oil. Leave to marinate for 30 minutes. Heat 1 tablespoon clarified butter in a wok and sweat the onion. Take the chicken pieces from the marinade, drain, and sear on all sides in the wok over a high heat. Add the spices and the chicken stock. Braise the curry over a low heat for 25–30 minutes, then remove and keep warm. Heat the remaining clarified butter in the wok, peel and halve the bananas lengthwise, and fry briefly. Add the warm chicken pieces, scatter with the chile rings, and heat through again. If desired, sprinkle with freshly shredded coconut and serve with rice.

STRIPS OF DUCK BREAST
WITH BEAN SPROUTS

Dishes in which the breast of the duck is used are considered delicacies even in China. As the meat is precooked, the remaining ingredients remain crispy.

Serves 4

| ¾ lb duck breast |
| 1⅓ cups fresh mung or soya bean sprouts |
| 1 scallion |
| 3 thin slices fresh ginger, 2½ tablespoons oil |
| For the Szechuan pepper oil: |
| 2 tablespoons peanut oil |
| 2 teaspoons Szechuan peppercorns |
| For the sauce: |
| ½ cup chicken broth (see pages 52–3) |
| 2 teaspoons rice wine, 2 teaspoons red wine vinegar |
| 2 garlic cloves |

Preheat the oven to 400°F and roast the duck breast until the meat is still pink. Cool and remove the fatty skin. Briefly blanch the bean sprouts in boiling water, drain, and cool. Cut the scallion into thin slices. Cut the ginger slices and the garlic for the sauce into fine strips. To make the Szechuan pepper oil, heat the oil in a wok until it boils. Roughly crush the peppercorns, add, and cook for about 1 minute. Allow the oil to cool, pour out, and reserve. Make the dish as described in the picture sequence.

Preparation: First cut the roast duck breast into thin slices, then into fine strips.

Method:

Bring the oil to a boil in a wok with the onion and the ginger. Remove from the heat, leave to stand for 5 minutes, then remove the onion and ginger.

Heat the oil again until it boils. Add the bean sprouts and fry for a few seconds, stirring and turning constantly.

Add the strips of duck meat. It is particularly important to keep all the ingredients moving constantly.

Mix the ingredients for the sauce together thoroughly, pour into the wok, and heat very quickly. Arrange and pour the Szechuan pepper oil over the dish.

Stir-frying
The wok makes it easy

Rapid cooking over a high heat while constantly stirring requires only a little fat. The meat and vegetables become crisp and crunchy. The wok can also be used occasionally for deep-frying, as in the recipe to the right.

DICED DUCK MEAT WITH GREEN PEPPER

It is best to use the breast of the duck for such dishes. If desired, however, you can also use leg meat, in which case the cooking time is longer.

Serves 4

¾ lb duck breast with skin
1 egg white
2 tablespoons and 1 teaspoon cornstarch
¼ teaspoon salt
1 large green pepper
2¼ cups vegetable oil
For the spice mixture:
ginger
2 tablespoons light soy sauce
2 teaspoons rice wine
1½ teaspoons sugar
½ cup chicken broth (see pages 52–3)
1 teaspoon sesame oil
pinch each of salt and freshly ground white pepper

Beat the egg white until stiff. Mix together the ingredients for the spice mixture. Make the dish as shown in the picture sequence.

Preparation: Cut the duck meat into ¾-inch cubes. Beat the egg white. Mix with 2 tablespoons cornstarch and the salt in a bowl, and add the cubes of meat. Halve the pepper, remove the stalk and seeds, and cut into ½-inch squares.

Method:

Bring the oil to a boil in a wok, allow to cool a little, add the duck meat, deep-fry for about 3 minutes and remove.

Add the diced pepper to the oil and cook until it discolors slightly. Remove and drain.

Pour off most of the oil, leaving 2 tablespoons. Add the spice mixture and heat. Add the diced meat and pepper, and cook while stirring.

Mix the remaining cornstarch in cold water to make a thin liquid, add to the dish, allow to thicken slightly, and then serve.

Preparation: Pour the marinade over the meat and leave for 20 minutes. Fry the chile pieces and the Szechuan pepper on a wire-mesh spoon in the hot oil until crisp, and reserve.

MARINATED CHICKEN WITH PEANUTS

Contrasting flavors give this chicken dish its particular character: on the one hand, the spiciness of the marinade, which is dominated by the heat of the chiles and the special flavor of Szechuan pepper, and on the other hand the sweetish taste of peanuts.

Serves 4

¾ lb skinless chicken breast
2–3 dried chile peppers
1 teaspoon Szechuan peppercorns
2 scallions
2–3 celery stalks
1–1½-inch piece fresh ginger
2 garlic cloves
oil for frying
¾ cup shelled peanuts
For the marinade:
1 tablespoon rice wine
1 tablespoon light soy sauce
½ teaspoon salt

1 teaspoon cornstarch
For the sauce:
1 cup chicken broth (see pages 52–3)
1 tablespoon light soy sauce
1 teaspoon sugar
2 teaspoons lemon juice
1½ teaspoons cornstarch

Cut the meat into ¾-inch cubes. Remove the seeds from the chile peppers and cut the flesh into pieces. Roughly crush the peppercorns. Shred the scallions, the celery, and the ginger, and cut the garlic into thin slices. To make the marinade, mix together the rice wine, the soy sauce, the salt, and the cornstarch. Mix together the ingredients for the sauce. Heat the oil in the wok until it boils, then follow the directions in the picture sequence.

To make the diced chicken:

Add the diced meat to the wok and deep-fry until it is white and firm. Then remove quickly.

Deep-fry the peanuts until they are light brown. Remove and drain on paper towels.

Pour out most of the oil, leaving 2½ tablespoons. Heat the oil remaining in the wok and briefly sauté the scallions, celery, ginger, and garlic.

Add the meat, chiles, and Szechuan pepper. Pour in the spice sauce and allow to thicken while stirring.

Simmer for about 1 minute while stirring. Mix in the peanuts and serve with rice.

Bone the chicken breast and cut the meat into fine strips. In a bowl, mix the egg white and the cornstarch, then stir in the meat. Wash the peppers, remove the seeds and pith, and cut the flesh into thin strips. Halve the chile pepper lengthwise, remove the seeds and finely chop the flesh. Cut the bamboo shoots into similarly thin strips. Heat the oil in a wok, fry the meat, remove, and drain well. Heat the peanut oil, fry the leek and the ginger while stirring, then add the pepper, chile, and bamboo shoots. As soon as the vegetables are soft, mix in the meat. Sprinkle with rice wine and soy sauce, and season with salt and sugar.

GINGER CHICKEN

Serves 4
one 3-lb chicken
salt
1 onion
1 garlic clove
2-inch piece fresh ginger
1 piece candied stem ginger
1 tablespoon oil
½ cup water
1 tablespoon ginger syrup
1 ripe beefsteak tomato
1 green pepper
freshly ground white pepper

Wash the chicken inside and out under running water, and pat dry. Cut into 20 pieces and rub with salt. Peel the onion and the garlic, and chop finely. Peel the ginger and cut into fine slices. Dice the candied ginger. Heat the oil in a wok and fry the legs and wings of the chicken for 10 minutes. Add the breast pieces and cook for 5 minutes. Add the onion, garlic, candied ginger, and fresh ginger, and fry. Add the water and the ginger syrup, and degrease the pan. Cover and braise the chicken over a low heat for 20 minutes.

In the meantime, scald the tomato with boiling water, skin and dice, removing the base of the stem and the seeds. Wash the green pepper, quarter, remove the seeds and pith, and cut the flesh into strips. Scatter the tomato and green pepper over the chicken and cook for a further 15 minutes. Season the chicken with salt and pepper. Serve with rice or unleavened bread.

CHICKEN WITH PEPPER AND BAMBOO SHOOTS

Serves 4
¾ lb chicken breast on the bone
½ egg white
1 teaspoon cornstarch
1 each green and red pepper
1 small chile pepper
1 cup bamboo shoots
oil for frying
2 tablespoons peanut oil
½ cup finely chopped leek
1½ teaspoon freshly chopped ginger
1 tablespoon rice wine
2 tablespoons light soy sauce
½ teaspoon salt
½ teaspoon sugar

Szechuan pepper
(*Xanthoxylum pipertum*) comes originally from western China. The peppercorn is often used whole and has a very spicy flavor.

SZECHUAN CHICKEN

Here is an outstanding example of the hot Chinese cuisine that is cherished in this part of China. You might think that the devilishly hot chile pepper would overwhelm the delicate flavor of the chicken. But far from it; the characteristic flavor of the chicken is, in fact, enhanced by the spicy heat of the chile.

Serves 4
one 3-lb chicken
½ teaspoon salt
1 teaspoon Szechuan peppercorns, roughly crushed
3 tablespoons light soy sauce, 1 level teaspoon cornstarch
1½–2 carrots
small bunch scallions
2–3 fresh red chile peppers
¼ cup vegetable oil

Wash the chicken inside and out under running water and pat dry with paper towels. Completely bone the chicken and cut the meat into bite-sized pieces of about equal size. Place in a dish, sprinkle with salt and the Szechuan pepper, and sprinkle with the soy sauce. Sift the cornstarch on top, cover, and marinate for 30 minutes.

Clean the carrots and scallions and cut into thin 2-inch long strips. Halve the chile peppers lengthwise, seed, and cut the flesh into thin slices. Heat half of the oil in a wok and stir-fry half of the marinated meat for 2–3 minutes until crisp and light brown, remove immediately, and keep warm. Stir-fry the remaining meat in the same way, and remove. Add the rest of the oil to the wok and briefly stir-fry the vegetables and the chiles. Add the meat, heat everything together, and mix well. Add further soy sauce as desired, and serve with rice or noodles.

Variation: You can prepare duck in the same way. Completely bone a 3½-lb duck and remove most of the visible fat. Remove the skin and fat from the breast, and cut the meat into evenly sized dice. Use the same spices and vegetables as in the chicken recipe, and follow the same method. Season with plenty of chopped cilantro.

Chicken fried in pastry

A *variation on egg rolls*

For this dish, you can use either ready-made egg roll pastry, or, as shown here, phyllo pastry. The wafer-thin pastry should be handled carefully, as it dries out very quickly and becomes brittle. Keep it moist with water or brush it with oil. Cover pastry not being used with a damp dishtowel. You can vary the vegetables for the filling as desired.

Serves 4 as an appetizer
¾ oz dried Chinese mushrooms
½ cup canned bamboo shoots
½ cup peas
1-inch piece fresh ginger
1 bunch chives
3 sheets phyllo pastry
½ lb skinless chicken breast

peanut oil for frying
For the marinade:
1 tablespoon dark soy sauce
½ teaspoon salt
1 tablespoon rice wine
freshly ground white pepper
1 teaspoon sesame oil
1 teaspoon cornstarch

Soak the dried mushrooms; as soon as they have acquired their normal shape, drain, and press out lightly so that they are not too damp. Cut the bamboo shoots into fine strips. Cook the peas in boiling salted water until soft. Finely chop the ginger and the chives. To make the marinade, mix the ingredients together in a bowl. Cut the pastry into 5-inch squares, fill them with the chicken mixture, and fry them in the hot oil, as shown in the picture sequence.

To fry the chicken in pastry:

Cut the chicken breasts diagonally into equally thin slices

Remove the stalks from the soaked and drained mushrooms and cut the caps into fine strips.

Pour the marinade over the meat, the prepared vegetables, ginger, and chives, and leave to infuse.

Place the filling on the pastry squares. Fold the pastry first into a triangle and then like an envelope.

Heat the oil in the wok, fry the parcels for about 4 minutes, turning several times.

Beggar's chicken

The chance invention of a poor man

This story about beggar's chicken has been handed down for generations, and is as enchanting as a fairy tale. Once upon a time there was a poor man from the Chinese province of Anhuei, who, driven by hunger, stole a chicken. While he sat happily by the side of a lake and kindled a fire, a feudal lord came riding by. Startled by the appearance of the nobleman and his armed escorts, the poor man covered the stolen chicken with mud from the lake and threw it into the fire. As fate would have it, the nobleman alighted from his horse to warm himself by the fire. It was a long time before he moved on. By now the chicken was covered with a hard, burned layer of clay. Furious, the poor man threw a stone against the casing, whereupon it broke open, releasing an incomparable aroma. Beggar's chicken is still cooked this way today. Stuffed with exquisite ingredients, wrapped in lotus leaves, encased in clay, and cooked in a coal fire, it has become a speciality known throughout the world.

Traditionally, the chicken, which has been stuffed and spiced with cardamom, ginger, chile, cilantro, and garlic, is wrapped in lotus leaves, tied up tightly, and then encased in clay. The Chinese also mix finely chopped rice straw into the clay. Later, they break open the baked clay with hard, sharp blows of an ax to reveal the incomparably juicy chicken.

BEGGAR'S CHICKEN

This version of the original recipe, is made in a clay pot without the coating of mud. The pot must, however, be hermetically sealed with a flour-and-water paste in order to achieve a result that comes close to the original. If you can find lotus leaves in an Asian shop, and are not afraid of the work involved in making the clay casing, you are warmly encouraged to use the old method; for this, the chicken must be cooked at a far higher temperature, at least 425°F.

Serves 4
one 3¾-lb chicken
1 teaspoon salt, 10 peppercorns
½ teaspoon cardamom seeds
1 teaspoon freshly grated ginger
2 small chile peppers
1 tablespoon freshly chopped cilantro
1 garlic clove, peeled
For the stuffing:
2 shallots
5 oz Chinese cabbage
3 tablespoons vegetable oil
½ cup finely chopped bamboo shoots
2 tablespoons dark soy sauce
Also:
1 stem lemon grass
1 star anise
1 celery stalk
2 cups flour
water

Preheat the oven to 350°F. Soak the clay pot in lukewarm water. Wash the chicken inside and out, and dry well. In a mortar, grind the salt with the peppercorns and the cardamom. Add the ginger, chiles, cilantro, and garlic, and work into a paste. Spread some of the paste over the inside of the chicken and rub the remainder into the skin.

To make the stuffing, peel and dice the shallots, and roughly chop the Chinese cabbage. Heat the oil in a wok and stir-fry the shallots and Chinese cabbage for 2–3 minutes. Add the bamboo shoots and the soy sauce. Use this to stuff the chicken and close the opening with a toothpick. Place the chicken in the well-soaked clay pot and add the lemon grass, star anise, and celery. Work the flour and water into a soft paste, spread it along the edge of the pot, and place the lid on top. Apply more paste to the outside, so that the pot is completely sealed. Cook in the oven for 2 hours. To serve, carefully open the pot with a knife. Serve with rice and rice pancakes.

Fresh chickens are always live chickens in Asian markets. Expertise is therefore required when buying, for the plumage can also conceal inferior quality.

HAINAN CHICKEN WITH RICE

This recipe from the island of Hainan in the South China Sea has become widespread. Various versions of it are cooked throughout the world, wherever the Chinese have settled. It is a light dish, which can be made hotter by the addition of a chile pepper.

Serves 4

one 3½-lb chicken
2 teaspoons salt
1 teaspoon oyster sauce
1 garlic clove, crushed
6¼ cups water
1 scallion
2–2½ sliced celery stalks
1 tablespoon and 1 teaspoon finely chopped fresh ginger
1 fresh red chile pepper, seeded and chopped (optional)
1 cup rice
¼ cup coconut milk
1 cup chicken broth (see pages 52–3)
1 tablespoon finely chopped onion
½ head iceberg lettuce

Wash the chicken inside and out and carefully pat dry. Rub the salt, oyster sauce, and garlic into the inside and on the outside of the chicken, cover with foil, and leave to stand for 60 minutes. Place the scallion, the celery, 1 tablespoon of the ginger, and, if desired, the chile pepper in the water and bring to a boil. Place the chicken in the liquid and cook for 45– 55 minutes, until tender. Cook the rice with the coconut milk, the chicken broth, the onion, and the remaining ginger over a low heat until *al dente*. Remove the chicken from the hot broth, remove the bones, and cut all the meat or just the breasts into pieces of equal size, and arrange on the lettuce. Serve the rice and the chicken broth, including the cooked vegetables, alongside. Serve with a soy sauce and, if liked, a chile or radish sauce.

FIVE COLORS SOUP

We would describe this substantial soup as a stew, and it can certainly be served as one. It can also be served in small portions as part of a Chinese meal.

Serves 4

2 chicken legs, about 6 oz each
8 quail eggs
4 scallops
2 oz belly of pork
¾ oz dried Chinese mushrooms
⅓ cup bamboo shoots
½ lb bok-choi
½ leek
¼ cup dark soy sauce
peanut oil for frying
1 oz rice stick noodles
1 tablespoon peanut oil
1 tablespoon rice wine
freshly ground white pepper
4½ cups boiling chicken broth (see pages 52–3)

Bring some water to a boil in a steamer. Wash the chicken legs, cut into bite-sized pieces, and place in a flameproof dish with the quail eggs. Cook in the steamer for 5 minutes. Remove, shell the eggs, and drain the meat well. Take the scallops from the shells and clean well. Cut the belly of pork into strips 2–2½ inches long. Soak the mushrooms and drain well, remove the stalks, and cut the caps into thin strips. Cut the bamboo shoots into thin slices. Halve the Chinese leaves lengthwise, cut them into 2-inch long pieces and then diagonally into thin strips. Cut the leek into batons 1¼ inches long. Make the soup as described in the picture sequence.

To make the five colors soup: Sprinkle the steamed chicken pieces and quail eggs evenly with 2 tablespoons of soy sauce and leave to infuse for 15 minutes.

Heat the oil in a wok, fry the chicken pieces and eggs until golden brown, and remove carefully.

Pour boiling water over the rice noodles. Drain as soon as they are soft. Cut smaller as required.

Heat the peanut oil and brown the leek. Add 1 tablespoon each of rice wine and soy sauce, season with pepper, and add the boiling broth.

Place the cabbage leaves in a flameproof casserole and then distribute all the ingredients except the scallops on top.

Remove the leek from the broth and pour the broth over the layered ingredients. Bring the soup to a boil.

Reduce the heat and simmer until everything is almost soft. Add the scallops and continue to cook for a few minutes.

Boiled chicken

Part of almost every national cuisine in Asia

Boiled chicken is very popular in Asian cooking generally, and especially in Chinese cuisine. There are a great many recipes with boiled chicken: as a soup, which in Chinese meals is served last, or as a stew, which is served as a main course and is only seldom accompanied by other courses. Vegetables of all types, as well as rice or noodles, are used as additional soup ingredients.

CHICKEN STEW WITH NOODLES

This is a substantial main course with vegetables and noodles, which, served in small portions, can also be used as a soup course.

Serves 4

one 1¾-lb chicken
5 oz. (4 cups) fresh leaf spinach
2–3 celery stalks
1 large leek
1-inch piece fresh ginger, thinly sliced
2 tablespoons rice wine
1–2 teaspoons salt
2¼ cups water or chicken stock
8 oz Chinese egg noodles
7 oz shiitake mushrooms
1 tablespoon light soy sauce

Make the stew as shown in the picture sequence. Before serving, take the meat off the bones and cut into pieces.

To make the noodle soup with chicken: Blanch the washed chicken in boiling water for 4–5 minutes, remove, rinse with cold water, and drain.

Wash the spinach and dry well. Remove the stalks and cut the leaves evenly into sections about 1½ inches long.

Place the chicken, celery, leek, and ginger in a pot, add the rice wine, salt, and water or stock.

Bring to a boil quickly over a high heat, reduce the heat, and simmer for 1 hour, skimming frequently.

Cook the noodles until *al dente*. When the chicken is cooked, remove the ginger and leek, add the noodles and cook briefly.

In a separate saucepan, cook the mushrooms in salted water for about 10 minutes. Add to the soup with their cooking liquid about 15 minutes before the end of the cooking time

Add the spinach to the soup 5 minutes before the end of the cooking time and continue to cook, making sure that the spinach remains crisp. Season with the soy sauce.

CHICKEN SOUP WITH RADISH

This combination may appear somewhat strange at first, but it will win you over with its fine taste.

Serves 4

4 chicken wings, about 1 lb
2 chicken legs, about 1 lb
3 carrots
¾ lb white radish or daikon
1 leek
3 oz rice stick noodles
1-inch piece fresh ginger, thinly sliced
9 cups chicken broth (see pages 52–3)
1 tablespoon rice wine
2 tablespoons light soy sauce
1¼ teaspoons salt
freshly ground white pepper
1 tablespoon freshly chopped cilantro

Carefully wash the chicken pieces, dry, and cut each into 3–4 large pieces with the bones. Wash and peel the carrots and radish. Make the soup as described below. Cook the rice noodles in salted water until soft and rinse with cold water. Add to the soup and reheat.

To make the chicken soup: Cut the carrots into batons ¼ inch thick and 1½ inches long. Cut the radish into ¼-inch thick slices, and cut these into quarters.

Peel the ginger, cut into slices, and crush with a knife. Cut the leek in half lengthwise and then into quarters.

Place the chicken meat, leek, and ginger in the broth and bring to a boil. Skim off the foam frequently.

After 15 minutes of cooking, add the carrots and the radish, bring back to a boil and simmer gently for a further 30 minutes.

Carefully mix the rice wine, soy sauce, salt, and pepper, and add to the broth. Add the noodles and cilantro and heat through.

Yakitori
Japanese delicacies

As an hors d'oeuvre, a snack, or a kebab for barbecuing, these colorful compositions of different ingredients enjoy great popularity not only in Japan. The basic ingredient is chicken, but you can vary the dish by serving it with a wide range of accompaniments.

Serves 4
¼ lb chicken skin
¼ lb chicken livers
¼ lb chicken gizzards
½ lb boneless chicken drumstick
1 each yellow and red pepper
4 scallions
For the yakitori sauce:
10 oz chicken bones
1¾ cups dark soy sauce
1¾ cups mirin (sweet rice wine)
1 cup sake
¼ cup sugar
¼ cup dark soy sauce
For the chicken balls:
1 cup finely chopped chicken breast
1 small beaten egg
1 teaspoon freshly grated ginger
1 tablespoon cornstarch, dissolved in 2 tablespoons water
To season:
ground sansho (Japanese pepper)
salt
mustard
lemon wedges
Also:
16 bamboo skewers

To make the sauce, roast the bones in the oven at 400°F for about 35 minutes until golden brown. In the meantime, prepare the meat and the vegetables:

boil the skin until soft, carefully wash the chicken livers, remove the tough skin from the gizzards, wash the vegetables, and seed the peppers. To make the chicken balls, place the finely chopped chicken in a food processor and purée. Prepare the kebabs and cook as described in the picture sequence. Before serving, dip once more in the yakitori sauce.

Place the roasted bones with the ingredients for the yakitori sauce in a saucepan and reduce by about one quarter.

Cut the chicken skin, giblets, leg meat, and vegetables into 1-inch squares.

Place the various ingredients on the skewers, mixing the meat, skin, and vegetables.

Mix the puréed meat with the other ingredients for the chicken balls, knead well, and shape into 1-inch balls.

Broil or grill the kebabs on both sides, immerse in the yakitori sauce, and cook again until it has been absorbed.

Place the balls in very gently boiling water, allow to rise, remove after 2–3 minutes, and leave to cool.

For the coating:

2 egg whites

2 tablespoons cornstarch

¼ teaspoon salt

2 tablespoons chopped scallions with some
of the green part

1 tablespoon freshly chopped ginger

Cut the meat into 1¼-inch squares ½-inch thick.
Make the dish as shown in the picture sequence.
To serve, arrange the chicken with the diamond-
shaped pieces of pepper and the lemon wedges.

Preparation: Mix together the ingredients for the spice mixture and marinate the cut meat in it for 30 minutes. Remove the seeds and the pith from the peppers and cut the flesh into diamond-shaped pieces.

To make the fried chicken:

Whip the egg white until frothy and mix in the cornstarch. Add the salt, scallion, and ginger.

Turn the meat in the cornstarch, tap to remove any excess, then dip in the egg-white mixture.

JAPANESE FRIED CHICKEN TATSUTA

Fall colors characterize this dish, which was named after the river Tatsuta in Japan. Here fall unfurls its colorful splendor in the famous maple woods. The chicken marinated in soy sauce displays the same varied tints, and in Japan the peppers are even cut into the shape of maple leaves.

Serves 2–4

1 lb skinless chicken breast	
1 each red, green and yellow pepper	
cornstarch for coating	
vegetable oil for frying	
salt	
4 lemon wedges	
For the spice mixture:	
2 tablespoons dark soy sauce	
2 tablespoons sake	
1 teaspoon freshly grated ginger	

Heat the oil in a wok, add the meat, fry until crisp, then remove and drain.

Fry the pepper diamonds until they are soft on the outside, but for no longer than 30 seconds. Remove and season with salt.

Cold delicacies

The display of an array of cold foods, long ago a tradition in the houses of the nobility and, later, the upper middle classes, was, to a large extent, used to flaunt the talents of the chefs, who evidently took great pleasure in making their cold creations true works of art. Reading very old cookbooks, we may marvel at the way in which cold poultry was transformed into pies, terrines, and exquisite galantines, the latter mostly in the original shape of the bird. Today, cold poultry dishes are as delicious as ever, and although they are no longer presented in the same flamboyant way, a little decorative flourish is still welcome.

To many people foie gras of goose and duck are the epitome of cold poultry dishes, but other, less expensive, delicacies exist too. Poultry is immensely versatile, combining perfectly with ingredients of subtle flavor as well as with strong spices. It can be served as hors d'oeuvres, with salads, and as main courses.

Poultry liver pâté in brioche dough with a filling of *foie gras* and truffle
— an example of the cuisine of our times, when good taste and tradition coincide.

The rice salad should be dressed at least 1 hour before serving. Garnish with halved cherry tomatoes.

Chicken, quail, and duck liver

Poultry salads as appetizers and as substantial main courses

The size of salads varies, depending on whether they are to be served as an appetizer or a main course. For exquisite salads, the rule of thumb is: the finer the ingredients, the smaller the portions.

RICE SALAD WITH BOILED CHICKEN

You can also make this dish with a roast chicken, which, even without the brown skin, gives the salad a hearty note.

Serves 2–4
1 tablespoon vegetable oil
1 tablespoon finely diced onion
1 small garlic clove, crushed
½ cup long-grain rice
2¼ cups light chicken stock (see pages 52–3)
salt, freshly ground white pepper
35 saffron threads
½ lb cooked chicken without skin and bones
5 oz. cooked green asparagus
½ cup chopped cooked celery
2½ cups sliced mushrooms, about 5 oz.
For the salad dressing:
¼ cup mayonnaise
¼ cup crème fraîche, 1 tablespoon light soy sauce
salt, freshly ground white pepper
2 tablespoons chicken stock
1 tablespoon chopped fresh parsley

Heat the oil in a saucepan, sweat the onions and garlic, add the rice and continue to cook briefly. Add the chicken stock, salt, pepper, and saffron threads. Cook until soft, as for a risotto, and allow to cool. Chop the chicken and asparagus, and mix into the rice with the celery and mushrooms. Mix together the ingredients for the dressing, pour on the salad, and toss.

SALAD WITH WARM QUAIL
Serves 4

two 5-oz quails

salt, freshly ground white pepper

2 sprigs fresh thyme, 2 tablespoons peanut oil

1 tablespoon sesame seeds, ½ cup purslane

¼ head curly endive, 8 cherry tomatoes

For the vinaigrette:

2 tablespoons sherry vinegar

½ teaspoon strong mustard

salt, some pink peppercorns

1 tablespoon finely chopped scallion

¼ cup peanut oil, 1 small chile pepper

Preheat the oven to 400°F. Season the quails with salt and pepper, and place 1 sprig of thyme in the stomach cavity of each. Heat the oil in a roasting pan, brown the quails on all sides, sprinkle with the sesame seeds, and roast for 20–25 minutes. In the meantime, wash the purslane and the curly endive, dry, and arrange on 4 plates. Cut the still warm quails into quarters and arrange two quarters alongside each portion of salad, garnishing with halved cherry tomatoes. Mix the ingredients for the vinaigrette together. Halve and seed the chile pepper, slice, and add to the salad dressing. Sprinkle the vinaigrette over the salad and the quails.

DUCK LIVER
WITH TWO KINDS OF ENDIVE

This salad can also be made with the livers of chicken or turkey.

Serves 4

½ lb duck liver

1 tablespoon vegetable oil

2 teaspoons finely chopped shallots

1½ tablespoons unsalted butter, 2 teaspoons chopped fresh parsley

salt, freshly ground white pepper

1 each white and red endive

4 tablespoons soya bean sprouts

For the vinaigrette:

2 tablespoons cider vinegar, 1 pinch curry powder

salt, freshly ground white pepper

3 tablespoons peanut oil, 1 tablespoon walnut oil

Wash the liver under cold running water and cut into pieces. Heat the oil in a frying pan and briefly sweat the shallot. Add the liver and sear. Add the butter and the parsley, and finish cooking the liver, stirring constantly. Season with salt and pepper. Cut the endives into individual leaves, wash, dry, remove part of the bitter base and cut the leaves lengthwise into strips. Arrange with the lukewarm livers on 4 plates and sprinkle the soya bean sprouts over them. Mix together all the ingredients for the vinaigrette and drizzle it over the salad and liver.

Roast poultry is the highlight of these fresh summer salads.

Foie gras
The controversial delicacy

The liver of the goose is, as in other types of poultry, among the finest cuts that the bird has to offer. The liver of the goose (or duck) becomes a delicacy, albeit a highly controversial one, only when it comes from force-fed animals. And it is here that the opinions of animal rights supporters and gourmets diverge. Animal rights supporters portray the force-feeding of geese as torture, but anyone who observes this procedure critically will see that these highly sensitive animals remain unperturbed by it. Stressed geese produce liver of poor quality, which would be bad for trade; for this reason alone it

In the Périgord, in France, Madame rears the gray geese with the "golden liver." In spite of the plentiful supply of *foie gras* from this and other parts of France, and from Poland, Hungary, and Israel, the increasing demand leads to ever rising prices.

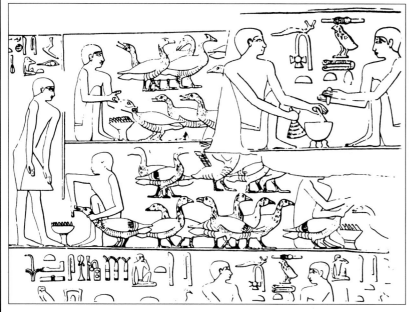

Force-feeding of geese 4,500 years ago. A representation from the tomb of a high Egyptian functionary named Ti. This is one of many pieces of evidence that prove that this method of fattening is no modern invention.

is logical that the producers should handle their geese very cautiously. Compared with other types of poultry, which are intensively farmed in factory environments, geese, which range freely outdoors, enjoy a life that is largely characteristic of their species.

People long ago developed methods of fattening poultry that were intended as food. This was certainly done to achieve more weight in the form of meat and fat. The fact that such intensive fattening also caused the liver to increase in size was a palatable side effect. As far back as 2500 BC the Egyptians recognized that the goose, a bird of passage, becomes very voracious in order to gather energy for long flights, and put this natural tendency to use for fattening the geese they reared. Since that time, scientific experiments have shown that when unlimited amounts of feed are made available, geese eat more than is given to them during regulated force-feeding. The ancient Romans, who were

The *marchés au gras* sell the full range of *foie gras*. From November to March, these markets are the emporia for livers in the southwest of France.

The range is wide, and before purchase each liver is thoroughly checked by the shrewd public. An indentation left after pressing with a finger confirms quality.

highly inventive in culinary practices, also discovered how to obtain particularly fine *foie gras*. They fed flour balls made of barley, softened white bread, and figs or dates to geese, and to ducks and even peacocks, to produce large livers, so gourmets were able to appreciate this delicacy even in classical times.

Nowadays the *foie gras* market is dominated by France. The center of *foie gras* production is in southwest France, with the best quality livers coming from the Périgord and Gascogny. Additional supplies are provided mainly by Hungary, Poland, and Israel. The market is growing slowly but constantly. France itself is experiencing the greatest growth, and domestic production has long since ceased to be sufficient. But nature imposes quantitative limits on this sensitive fattening method, which can be carried out only manually. There is, therefore, no danger of mass production, and *foie gras* will always remain a superior, and correspondingly expensive, product.

The term *foie gras* covers not just the product made from goose liver, known in full as *foie gras d'oie*; the product made from duck liver — *foie gras de canard* — has already won a considerable market share, and is acclaimed and appreciated by connoisseurs for its powerful flavor.

Fresh or preserved?

Which is better: fresh liver or a processed product? Fresh, of course, says the gourmet, if it can be obtained. Raw liver that has been marinated for twenty-four hours is a real delight. The only reason to process it into a terrine, although this can be just as great a delicacy, is that not every gourmet has the opportunity to buy fresh liver. Force-feeding of geese is not permitted in many countries, and the liver of geese raised naturally, while good, is just not the same.

In France breeders sell fresh goose liver at the markets. The livers, between 1½ and 2 pounds in weight, come from geese weighing 13–17½ pounds. The amateur would probably find it somewhat difficult to check the quality of a fresh liver, but professionals and top chefs know what to look for. A good quality liver cannot necessarily be recognized by its color, which can vary from light beige to pink depending on the type of feed. It is the consistency that the purchaser looks at. The liver consists of two firm lobes, which, after careful separation, do not fit together again like rubber. The final criteria involves pressing the liver with the thumb or index finger, which should leave an indentation.

Removing the liver: A force-fed goose has to be cut up carefully to avoid damaging the liver. It is cut open along the breastbone and the meat is detached from the ribcage. Then the carcass is lifted off, and the liver is exposed and carefully removed.

Quality test: When the liver is pressed with the thumb, the depression must remain visible.

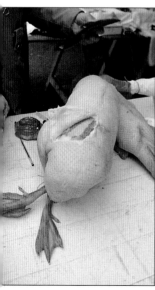

The liver can be sold with the goose. People buying it this way must also be able to check its quality, so a "window" is cut into the skin.

Truffles are the second most important ingredient for a *terrine de foie gras,* and therefore they can always be found among the range of products at a *marché au gras.*

Good quality fresh livers are smooth and firm. Only the best and consistent quality is accepted for the production of terrines. The right color is light but not whitish, for that indicates too high a fat content.

A comparison of a *foie gras* of goose and a *foie gras* of duck. The duck liver shown here (left) weighs 1½ pounds. It was vacuum-packed and has reddish marks from the remains of blood that has leaked from the veins. The 2-lb goose liver was transported packed in ice. It is not always possible to distinguish between goose liver and duck liver solely on the basis of color, as this is heavily dependent on the fat content and the feed. In general, however, the livers of ducks are yellowish, while those of geese are amber to whitish.

Using your thumb, break down the inside of the liver pieces a little. Proceed carefully so as not to pull them to pieces.

To clean the *foie gras*:

The liver must be at room temperature. Using only your hands, carefully break it in half. Check each half individually.

Carefully expose the visible tiny veins with the fingers, following the various branches of veins individually.

Care should be taken if green marks are visible on the liver. These come from gall, and they and a large part of the surrounding area must be cut out.

Remove the sinews and pads of fat at the start of the gall bladder, cutting out a wide area around, as remains of gall may be concealed underneath.

Pull out the blood vessels. They should be removed as fully as possible, so that the liver cannot become discolored by blood remains.

Carefully and completely pull or scrape off the thin skin of the liver with the blunt side of a knife, working toward the tip of the liver.

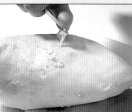

Reassemble the cleaned liver and return it to its original shape. It can now be used as required.

Foie gras of duck and goose

Which is better?

Many gourmets rank the flavor of goose liver above that of duck, but this says nothing about their true culinary merits; the somewhat more robust taste of duck liver also has its admirers. The quality of both depends to a large extent on the season; they are at their best in the winter. Animals slaughtered in the summer have smaller livers, with a lower fat content and a higher percentage of blood vessels; they are more suitable for frying than for the production of terrines. As *foie gras* is not cheap, leading chefs carry out a quality check before purchase. They cut off the tip of the liver and examine it for color changes. As *foie gras* is very sensitive to air and light, a gray border ¹⁄₁₀ to ¼-inch wide points to poor storage or to aging; in either case there will be a high degree of wastage during processing due to cleaning. If the liver is to be fried, a small slice should be tested; it should not melt away in the pan.

Ensuring that the *foie gras* arrive at their destination in good condition is vital. One of the main ways to package them for shipping is to wrap them in waxed paper and transport them in polystyrene containers filled with ice. Care needs to be taken to ensure that the ice does not melt and that the liver does not come into contact with light. The other method of dispatch is to vacuum-pack them. These packages have the disadvantage that when the air is sucked out, remains of gall from the bladder can be drawn out, and can then penetrate the blood vessels and spread widely through the tissue. Before use, the livers should be allowed to come up to room temperature under a damp cloth.

PARFAIT OF GOOSE LIVER

For this delicacy, you can use the tips of the liver or other pieces that become detached, for example, when you are removing the veins. They must be free of remains of blood and gall.

Serves 6–8

| 14 oz goose foie gras |
| 1½ tablespoons each red and white port |
| salt, freshly ground white pepper |
| 2 eggs, 1 cup lukewarm milk |
| 1 teaspoon soft unsalted butter for the terrine |

Reduce the port by half, and allow to cool. Make the parfait as shown in the picture sequence. A pinch of preserving salt can be added to avoid a rapid color change after turning out.

To make the parfait of goose liver:

Pressing lightly, push the liver pieces through a fine wood-framed sieve with a dough scraper.

Place the liver in a food processor, season with salt and pepper, and mix thoroughly, adding the eggs one at a time.

Pour in the milk in a thin stream and blend to a homogeneous paste.

Add the reduced alcohol, mix in well, and pour the mixture through a fine-mesh sieve.

Butter a terrine, pour in the liver mixture evenly without allowing bubbles to form. Cover with the lid.

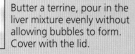

Place the terrine in a *bain-marie* with hot water (176°F) coming two-thirds of the way up its sides. Place on the bottom rack of a preheated 350°F oven. Check the temperature frequently.

The parfait will be fully cooked in 50 minutes. Allow it to cool and carefully remove the top layer with a pallet knife.

Using a tablespoon dipped in warm water, spoon out cones of parfait and arrange and serve as desired.

Terrine de foie gras
A culinary delight

It has not been proved that goose liver terrine really did originate in France, but it is undeniable that the French have a masterly understanding of its preparation. The quantities of ingredients used for this delicacy depend on the weight of the fresh liver. It will most often weigh around 1¾ pounds. To make a 1-quart terrine, you also need salt and pepper, 1 cup of vintage port, a dash of cognac and, if desired, 3½ ounces of cooked black truffles. The cooking time is 40–60 minutes in a *bain-marie* kept at 175°F. It is essential to control the temperature precisely to avoid the risk of contamination with staphylococcus bacteria. Cooking temperatures of only 100–140°F and cooking times of 30–40 minutes for a 2-pound terrine, as were recommended by some proponents of *nouvelle cuisine*, can be highly dangerous. You can use an instant-read meat thermometer to check that a core temperature of 175°F is maintained.

Monsieur Jean Legrand, an advocate of the classical method of preparing a *terrine de foie gras*, inspects the finished dish

1 Carefully open up the goose liver and remove any skin and veins that are still present.

2 Press the liver very carefully with the ball of your hand, and knead the individual pieces until soft.

3 Only salt and pepper are needed for seasoning, as the liver has a great deal of natural flavor.

4 Place the pieces of liver in a suitably large bowl and pour on the port and cognac.

5 Lightly massage in the marinade – do not press. Leave to infuse in a cool place for 24 hours.

6 Arrange the livers in layers and press lightly, so that there is no space between them.

7 Smooth the surface carefully with your hands and even out any hollows remaining.

8 Cover the terrine with a lid and cook in a *bain-marie* that has a constant temperature of 176°F.

9 Leave to rest in the terrine for 24 hours. Turn out and remove the excess fat.

FOIE GRAS PARFAIT WITH SNOW PEAS AND APPLE SALAD

Serves 8
foie gras *parfait (see pages 174–5)*
For the aspic cubes:
1½ cups poultry consommé (see pages 54–5)
pinch of salt, 2 teaspoons gelatin
For the salad:
1¾ cups snow peas, 2 tart apples
2 tablespoons sugar syrup, 1 tablespoon Calvados
juice of ½ lemon, 2 tablespoons crème fraîche
salt, freshly ground white pepper
6–8 small sprigs fresh chervil

Spoon out the desired number of cone shapes from the *foie gras* parfait. To make the aspic cubes, heat the consommé with the salt. Dissolve the gelatin in the hot consommé. Pour into a flat dish and chill to set.

To make the salad, blanch the snow peas in boiling salted water until *al dente*, and refresh with cold water. Peel and core the apples, and cut into batons. Place in a mixture of sugar syrup, Calvados, and lemon juice, and marinate for 5 minutes. Mix the *crème fraîche*, salt, and pepper with half the marinade. Add the batons. Arrange the snow peas with the apple salad, and garnish with chervil. Place the cones of parfait alongside. Cut the chilled aspic into cubes, place on the plates with the parfait and salad, and serve.

PRALINES OF FOIE GRAS OF GOOSE WITH PINK PEPPER CREAM

This recipe offers an attractive alternative way of serving the *terrine de foie gras*. Round scoops of terrine rolled in hazelnuts or pistachios delight the eye as well as the tastebuds.

Serves 4
¾ lb terrine de foie gras (see opposite page)
½ cup shelled, sliced hazelnuts
½ cup chopped pistachios
For the sauce:
6 tablespoons light cream, juice of ½ lime
pinch of salt, 1 tablespoon pickled pink peppercorns
For the garnish:
1 small curly endive

Using an ice cream scoop, make 8 equal-sized balls of *terrine de foie gras*. Smooth them by hand and chill them. Roast the hazelnuts if desired. To make the pralines, roll 4 of the balls in hazelnuts, and the other 4 in pistachios. Chill again.

To make the sauce, mix the cream and the lime juice, allow to thicken slightly, then season with salt and add the pink peppercorns.

Arrange the well-chilled pralines with the cream and garnish with a small bouquet of curly endive.

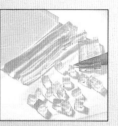

Aspic cubes: Turn the chilled aspic out onto waxed paper, cut into strips, and then into small dice.

To make the aspic:
Heat 2¼ cups of poultry consommé and dissolve 1 tablespoon gelatin in it. Add salt, pour into a deep baking pan, and leave to set. Dip the pan briefly in hot water, turn the aspic out onto waxed paper, cut into strips, and then into cubes.

STUFFED SQUAB LEGS

These morsels, their shape slightly reminiscent of cherries with stalks, make an unusual and delightful hors d'oeuvre. As the breasts are often cooked separately, this is an attractive way of using the tiny legs of squab, quail, or other types of small poultry.

Serves 4
8 squab legs
½ tablespoon sliced, roasted hazelnuts
3 oz poultry forcemeat (see recipe opposite)
salt, freshly ground white pepper
For poaching:
2¼ cups light poultry stock (see pages 52–3)
Also:
2 teaspoons unsalted butter
¼ cup poultry glaze (see pages 52–3)

To make the stuffing, roughly chop the hazelnuts and stir them evenly into the forcemeat. Bone and stuff the legs as shown in the picture sequence. Poach the finished packages in poultry stock with a temperature of 175°F for 25 minutes. Then remove, refresh in cold water, and allow to cool thoroughly. Coat the legs with the meat glaze (see recipe, right).

To stuff the squab legs:

Expose the thighbone, sever the knee joint, and detach half of the lower leg bone.

Season the inside of the legs with salt and pepper, and fill with the forcemeat using a pastry bag. Fold the skin over.

Brush suitably sized pieces of baking foil with melted butter. Place a leg on each, with the cut side facing down.

Wrap the legs not too tightly and twist the ends of the foil, pushing the packages into shape.

Stuffed poultry legs can be served attractively with aspic and a small salad garnish.

To stuff the quails:

Completely close the neck opening of the quails by sewing up the skin with fine kitchen string.

Using a spoon, carefully stuff the stomach cavity with the forcemeat and place a small truffle in each.

Do not stuff too full, as the forcemeat will expand during cooking. Sew up the stomach opening.

Tie the quails into shape with kitchen string, roll in baking film, and tie the ends.

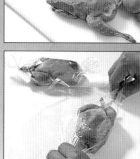

Poach the quail packages in the poultry stock with the bouquet garni and leave them to cool in the liquid.

Place the quails on a rack and coat them with glaze. Reheat any glaze that drips off and repeat the process.

Stuffed and served cold

Small stuffed birds can be served as single portions. Pieces of large birds, such as the legs, can also be stuffed. Skillful boning and stuffing will maintain the shape of the bird. Use your culinary imagination to create new and exciting stuffings.

STUFFED QUAILS

It is certainly time-consuming to stuff quails in this way, but — except for the glazing — the dish can be made a day in advance.

Serves 4 as an appetizer

four 5½-oz quails

For the forcemeat:

¼ lb dark or white poultry meat

salt, freshly ground white pepper

½ cup light cream, ¾ oz diced goose or duck foie gras

4 small truffles (about ⅓ oz each)

¼ cup shelled pistachios

For poaching:

6–9 cups light poultry stock (see pages 52–3)

1 bouquet garni

Also:

6–8 tablespoons poultry glaze (see pages 52–3)

Prepare the quails for stuffing as described on pages 40–1. Make sure the ingredients for the forcemeat are well chilled. Finely dice the meat, season well with salt and pepper, and purée to a stiff paste. Gradually mix in the cream and the *foie gras*. Chill the forcemeat. Pare the truffles thinly and halve the pistachios widthwise. Pass the forcemeat through a strainer, season, and mix in the pistachios. Stuff the quails, placing the truffles in the center. Truss the quails and wrap them in cooking film. Poach the quails in stock with a temperature of 176°F for 40 minutes. Leave to cool in the poaching liquid, take out of the film, and remove the string. Before glazing, chill well, so that the glaze adheres to the skin. As soon as the glaze has set, halve the stuffed quails lengthwise and arrange. Serve with cubes of aspic, as described far left.

Poultry mousse in aspic

The production of the finest mousses and aspics requires the best basic materials and careful techniques. Strong, full-bodied stocks are the basis for the mousses. With its sweetish taste, achieved by the addition of dessert wine, port, or Madeira, the aspic rounds off the powerful flavor of the mousse.

SQUAB MOUSSE IN GEWÜRZTRAMINER ASPIC

Serves 8 as an appetizer
For the aspic:
3¼ cups squab consommé (see pages 54–5)
1 cup Gewürztraminer wine, 1½ tablespoons gelatin
For the breasts:
2 squab breasts
salt, freshly ground white pepper
2 tablespoons vegetable oil, 8 leaves lemon balm
For the mousse:
1¾ cups dark squab stock (see pages 50–1)
½ bay leaf, 1 sprig thyme
6–8 white peppercorns, 1 clove, 3 whole allspice
1½ tablespoons Madeira, 2 teaspoons Grand Marnier
⅔ cup light cream, 3 tablespoons cold unsalted butter cubes
1½ teaspoons gelatin, ½ cup whipped cream
salt, freshly ground white pepper

This recipe is sufficient for 8 small molds, each holding approximately 6 tablespoons. Make the consommé from the squab carcasses and add the wine before clarifying. Dissolve the gelatin in the hot consommé. Lightly chill the molds before coating the insides with the gelatin mixture. As the gelatin begins to set quickly in iced water, do not chill too many molds at the same time, because they cannot be coated sufficiently quickly one after the other. If the gelatin coating is too thin, repeat the process. Chill the molds.

Preheat the oven to 350°F. Season the squab breasts with salt and pepper, and brown on both sides in the hot vegetable oil. Roast for 6–8 minutes, then allow to cool thoroughly. Remove the skin, cut the meat lengthwise into thin strips, and place in the molds as described opposite. Pour some of the remaining gelatin around the meat strips, so that the meat is firmly attached around the edge. Refrigerate the molds again. Make the mousse and fill the prepared molds as described opposite. Before serving, dip the molds briefly in hot water and turn out. Serve with fresh salad and a mild vinaigrette.

1 Fill only 4 molds with gelatin at the same time with jelly, ensuring that no air bubbles form.

2 Place the molds in iced water, allow to set briefly, then pour out most of the gelatin, leaving a thin coating in place.

3 To make the mousse, mix the stock with all the spices and the alcohol, and bring to a boil.

4 Simmer gently for 10 minutes, then add the cream, and boil down to a creamy consistency.

5 Remove the saucepan from the heat, add the diced butter, and beat with a hand-held mixer.

6 Pour the foaming sauce through a fine-mesh strainer and reserve in a bowl.

7 Dissolve the gelatin in warm water, and pour into the warm sauce, stirring constantly.

8 Chill until shortly before it sets, mix in the whipped cream, and season with salt and pepper.

9 Place 1 leaf of lemon balm and 3 slices of squab breast in each of the gelatin-lined molds.

10 Fill with mousse to ⅛-inch below the top of the molds, smoothing the surface.

11 As soon as the mousse has set, fill the molds to the top with gelatin, and cool thoroughly for 1–2 hours.

1 Spread the duck out on damp cheesecloth with the breast side flush with the edge, and season with salt and pepper. Spread the prepared forcemeat evenly over it.

2 Salt and pepper strips of *foie gras*, place in a line on the first third of the meat, and press lightly into the forcemeat.

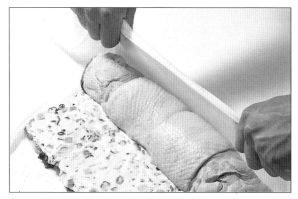

3 By lifting the cloth, roll up the galantine from the breast side toward the leg. The leg meat requires more heat than the breast.

4 It is important to keep the cloth taut when rolling the galantine, to avoid possible gaps between the skin and the forcemeat. Do not roll the cloth inside the meat.

5 Tie up the ends of the cloth with string and knot well. Do not tie the cloth too tightly, as the galantine will expand slightly during cooking.

6 Wrap the string around the roll at intervals of about 1¼ inches, looping it secure at each crossover; in this way the galantine keeps its shape.

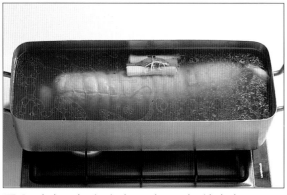

7 Poach the galantine in the poultry stock with the bouquet garni for about 60 minutes. It must always be covered by stock, which must have a constant temperature of 176°F.

8 Allow the galantine to cool in the stock, weighed down with a weight if necessary. Unwrap, remove any fat adhering to it, and slice.

A rolled galantine
A pâté with an unusual appearance

Modern galantines do not remotely resemble the original form from which they derive, for in the past these pâtés were presented in shapes that mimicked those of the birds whose meat they used. This was an art that required a great deal of effort, even if the leg bones and wing bones were left in place on the birds. But times changed, and the far more practical and easier-to-fill rolled pâté took its place in the kitchens of the top gastronomes. Free of all bones, the meat can be rolled, wrapping around and enclosing the flavorful forcemeat filling. The ingredients for a galantine must be well chilled; otherwise they cannot be worked into an emulsion.

Chicken galantine: the chicken has been made to resemble its original shape, as was the custom in times gone by.

GALANTINE OF DUCK
Serves 10
one 5½-lb duck
½ lb duck or chicken meat
salt, freshly ground white pepper
1 cup heavy cream
1½ tablespoons truffle juice from a jar
2 teaspoons cognac
2 tablespoons whipped cream
1 each duck liver and duck heart
2 teaspoons unsalted butter
¼ cup shelled pistachios
1 oz black truffles from a jar
5 oz cooked ham
3 oz foie gras of goose
Also:
2¼ cups light poultry stock (see pages 52–3)
1 bouquet garni

Bone the duck as described in the picture sequence on page 41. Dice the additional duck or chicken meat and chill. When well chilled, chop finely or pass through the fine disk of a meat grinder, and chill again thoroughly. Season the meat with salt and pepper, and purée finely in a food processor in several small portions. Gradually add the cream until a smooth forcemeat is produced. Chill this in a bowl set on ice. Then pass through a wood-framed sieve, place on ice again, and work in the truffle juice, the cognac, and the whipped cream. Finely dice the liver and heart, fry briefly in butter, and drain on paper towels. Halve the pistachios, finely dice the truffles, and cut the ham into ¼-inch dice. Cut the *foie gras* first into ½-inch thick slices and then into strips, and chill. Add the diced ingredients to the forcemeat, and stuff and roll the duck, as explained in the picture sequence opposite. The galantine can also be wrapped in baking foil and cooked.

Slices of the galantine can be attractively served with a salad garnish and aspic cubes.

Piquant and refreshing

Cold chicken breasts in aspic or with spicy sauces

Roasted or poached chicken leftovers can be transformed into other fine dishes. Used cold, for example, they make a fine addition to substantial salads made with potatoes, noodles, or various vegetables. In the following recipes, however, the poultry is prepared specially for the purpose, and only the best part — the breast meat — is used.

COLD DUCK BREAST WITH A HOT PEPPER VINAIGRETTE

Serves 4
2 skinless duck breasts, about ½ lb each
For the vinaigrette:
¼ cup raspberry vinegar
½ garlic clove, crushed
salt, freshly ground white pepper
¼ cup finely chopped shallots
1 small finely chopped chile pepper
½ cup chopped yellow and green peppers
3 tablespoons fine vegetable oil
Also:
1 small curly endive, lamb's-tongue lettuce

Prepare the duck breasts as in the following recipe and slice when cold. To make the vinaigrette, whisk all the ingredients together. Marinate the breast slices in the vinaigrette for about 15 minutes. Wash the curly endive and the lettuce, and dry. Arrange the duck slices in a fan shape, garnish with the lettuces, and pour the vinaigrette on top.

COLD DUCK BREAST WITH *SALSA VERDE*

A spicy appetizer for the summer months, this dish is typical of those made in the Italian region of Piedmont. When combined with the duck breast, the refreshing, slightly sour *salsa verde*, Italian for "green sauce," is a delight for the palate.

Serves 4 as an appetizer
2 skinless duck breasts, about ½ lb each
salt, freshly ground white pepper
3 tablespoons vegetable oil
¾ cup finely chopped shallots
½ cup dark poultry stock (see pages 50–1)
For the salsa verde:
2 teaspoons red wine vinegar
salt, freshly ground white pepper
½ cup olive oil
1 shallot, 1 garlic clove
3 tablespoons each finely chopped fresh curly and flat-leaf parsley
1½ tablespoons finely chopped fresh basil
2 anchovy fillets, finely chopped
2 cornichons, peeled and finely chopped
1½ teaspoons toasted pine nuts, 1½ teaspoons capers
To garnish:
lettuce leaves, quartered tomatoes

Season the duck breasts with salt and pepper, and prepare as described in the picture sequence. Preheat the oven to 350°F. After adding the poultry stock to the duck, place the casserole, uncovered, in the oven and cook for 25 minutes. Remove the breasts and allow to cool thoroughly. In the meantime, prepare the *salsa verde*. Mix all the ingredients together and leave to infuse well.

Heat the vegetable oil in a saucepan and brown the breasts. Add the shallots, sweat them until translucent, then pour in the chicken stock and complete the cooking. Cut the cooled duck breasts into thin slices with a sharp knife. Arrange the duck breast slices in a fan shape, garnish with lettuce leaves and tomato quarters and top with the *salsa verde*.

ROAST SQUAB BREASTS IN VEGETABLE BROTH

This dish is a refreshing delicacy in hot weather. The breasts are first cooked and then placed in a spicy lukewarm broth, and left to marinate overnight.

Serves 2 as an appetizer

4 squab breasts, wing bones attached
salt, freshly ground white pepper
3 tablespoons vegetable oil
For the broth:
½ cup white wine, 1 cup water
3 tablespoons white wine vinegar
6–8 peppercorns
2 cloves
1 bay leaf
3 whole allspice
2 sprigs fresh thyme
½ cup thinly sliced carrots
½ cup thinly sliced celery
½ onion, thinly sliced
⅓ teaspoon salt

Preheat the oven to 350°F. Brown the squab breasts as described in the picture sequence below and roast in the oven for 10 minutes. In the meantime, make the broth. Bring the white wine to a boil with the water, the vinegar, and the herbs and spices. Add the carrots, the celery, and the onion, and simmer gently for 10 minutes over a low heat. Set the broth aside, mix in the salt, and allow to cool slightly.

CHICKEN BRAWN WITH CARROTS AND CELERY

This recipe uses every part of the chicken: the breasts for the brawn, the legs for clarifying, and the bones, carcass, and skin for the stock.

Serves 4

one 2-lb chicken
1 bouquet garni
For clarifying:
1 carrot, 2 celery stalks
½ onion roasted in its skin, ½ garlic clove
1 bay leaf, 1 sprig of thyme
2 cloves, 6–8 peppercorns
a few dashes of balsamic vinegar
3 egg whites, 5 crushed ice cubes
Also:
1½ teaspoons gelatin
salt, freshly ground white pepper
3 tablespoons vegetable oil
¾ cup diced carrots, ¾ cup diced celery
4 sprigs fresh chervil

Cut the chicken into portions (see pages 24–5). Bone the legs and the breasts. Remove the skin from the legs, sever the knee joints, and remove the thigh bones. Make a stock from the bones, skin, carcass, and the bouquet garni, as described on pages 52–3. To clarify the stock, chop the thigh meat very finely and add to the stock with the clarifying ingredients. Boil down to 1 cup. Dissolve the gelatin in the reduced stock and allow to cool thoroughly. Preheat the oven to 350°F. Season the chicken breasts with salt and pepper, sear in hot oil, and roast for 10–12 minutes. Allow to cool, then pat dry with paper towels. Complete the brawn as described below.

Dip the molds briefly into hot water and turn out. Serve with the salad garnish.

Season the squab breasts with salt and pepper, brown in the hot oil, and complete the cooking in the oven. Allow to cool thoroughly. Make the broth, simmering the vegetables, herbs, and spices in the liquid. Pour the lukewarm broth over the cooled squab breasts, cover, and marinate overnight in the refrigerator. The following day, arrange the meat and vegetables on plates and serve with white bread.

Blanch the carrots and celery in boiling salted water, refresh with cold water, drain, and lay out to dry. Cut the roast chicken breasts into equal size dice. Pour lukewarm gelatin ⅛-inch deep into 4 timbale molds, place 1 tiny sprig of chervil in each, and let set. Mix the meat with the vegetables, fill the molds, and top up with the remaining gelatin. Cool thoroughly for 1–2 hours before turning out.

Confit

The term "confit" is used to describe pieces of meat preserved in salt and fat. Two methods of preservation must be used to turn duck or goose meat into this unmistakable southern French specialty, which is now an international favorite. It is an essential ingredient in many dishes, such as cassoulet and the vegetable soup known as *garbure*. To make a confit, first remove the fat from the stomach cavity of the ducks or geese, and reserve. Cut the birds into individual pieces. Rub with coarse salt or immerse in brine to protect the meat against spoilage and at the same time to draw out some of its natural juices. Sprinkle with dried herbs and refrigerate for 24 hours. After this time, carefully scrape the salt and herbs off the pieces of meat, and pat dry. Melt the duck or goose fat in a casserole and slowly braise the meat pieces, fully covered, over a low heat, stirring frequently. If necessary, add a little pork fat to reach the required quantity of fat. Depending on the age of the bird, the cooking time will be 1–2½ hours. Prepare an earthenware pot by first sterilizing it with boiling water, and then brushing the interior with melted fat, thereby making it airtight. Arrange the meat in layers alternating with melted fat. The top layer of meat must be covered with about 1¼ inches of fat. After the contents of the pot have cooled, fill up with fat, cover, and keep in a cool place for 3–4 weeks for the full flavor to develop. The confit will keep for about 4 months. Take out the meat in portions and on each occasion refill the pot with fat.

A fresh salad
of wild garlic and
curly endive is a good
accompaniment to the roulade.
It is dressed with a marinade consisting
of 3 tablespoons of olive oil, some balsamic vinegar
and 1 tablespoon of water, ¼ cup each of diced red and yellow
pepper, and 1 scallion cut into rings.

The pieces of goose are cooked in plenty of goose fat over a low heat.

Preserving with fat

With today's refrigeration technology being taken for granted, many methods of preservation have almost fallen into oblivion — unjustly, as many traditional recipes show. One method of preserving meat that has been known since time immemorial involves coating it with, or immersing it in, fat. For this, it is best to use types of meat that themselves have an excess of natural fat, such as geese and ducks. This method of preservation was developed by French peasants in the days before deep freezing to use the meat of the birds that had been bred exclusively for their *foie gras*.

To make the duck roulade:

Season the breasts with pepper, place the *foie gras* in position, and roll up; the pieces of meat should overlap.

Tie with kitchen string, looping it at each crossover and pulling each loop tight, as the roulade will shrink somewhat during smoking.

To prepare the duck breasts: Make an incision in the side of the duck breasts with a sharp knife, so that a pouch is formed. Gently beat flat and place next to each other.

Fully immerse the roulade in the prepared brine, cover with foil, and leave to infuse for 3 days.

Remove from the brine and soak fully immersed in cold water for half a day.

Pat the roulade dry, turn in sugar crystals, and hang up to dry for 1–2 days. Arrange for the roulade to be smoked.

The smoked roulade after slicing: the breast meat and the *foie gras* center make an attractive contrast.

SMOKED ROULADE OF DUCK BREAST AND *FOIE GRAS*

Serves 4

2 skinless duck breasts, about ¼ lb each

6 oz cleaned foie gras

salt, freshly ground white pepper

1 dash each port and cognac

For the brine:

4½ cups water

2 cloves, 6–8 peppercorns

½ bay leaf

1 small garlic clove

1 sprig fresh thyme, 2 whole allspice

zest of ½ orange and ½ lemon

½-inch piece fresh ginger

⅓ heaping cup coarse salt

Also:

preserving sugar

Prepare the duck breasts as illustrated in the picture sequence. Clean the *foie gras* (see pages 174–5), season lightly with salt and pepper, sprinkle with the port and cognac, and press into its original shape. The *foie gras* should be somewhat smaller than the breasts, so that it cannot run out. Make the roulade as shown. To make the brine, bring the water to a boil, add all the ingredients *except* the salt, and simmer gently for 15 minutes. Stir in the salt only after cooling. When smoking, ensure that the smoke is cold. After smoking for about 12 hours, remove the kitchen string and cut the roulade into thin slices.

Glossary of culinary terms

Bain-marie: A deep baking or roasting pan in which delicate foods, such as terrines, custards, and pâtés, are placed in hot water while cooking. The water comes about two-thirds of the way up the sides of the dish containing the food, and distributes the cooking heat of the oven or stove more gently and evenly.

Bake blind To bake a pastry case before it is filled. The pastry is usually lined with foil and filled with dried or baking beans to prevent the sides falling in and air bubbles forming during cooking.

Bard: To cover poultry or meat with slices of bacon or pork fat to prevent the flesh from drying out.

Blanch: To immerse food briefly in boiling water in order to prepare it, remove impurities or remove skin more easily.

Blanquette: Stew made without frying the meat first; a white ragout.

Bouquet garni: Small bunch of herbs, usually comprising parsley, thyme and bay leaf. It can also be made with vegetables and other herbs depending on the dish.

Braise: To sear and brown in hot fat, then add liquid and cook in a covered pot, often on a bed of vegetables. In a number of European countries the term also signifies stewing, steaming, or boiling for a short time.

Brioche: Unsweetened yeast dough, eaten as rolls or bread, and used for enclosing meat or pâtés to be baked.

Casserole: Flat, heavy roasting or braising pot with a lid; a dutch oven.

Chicken oyster: Oyster-shaped pieces of meat from the back of the chicken, the quality of which is equivalent to that of the fillet.

Clarify: To remove particles and other impurities from food.

Consommé: Particularly strong, clear meat broth.

Deep-fry: To fry in abundant hot fat until golden.

Essence: Concentrated reduced stock.

Extract: Reduced essence.

Forcemeat: Puréed meat, fish or vegetables that is well seasoned and bound, and used as a filling or stuffing for pâtés, terrines, galantines, cuts of meat, poultry, fish or vegetables.

Fricassee: Stewed or fried pieces of meat served in a thick white sauce.

Galantine: Dish made from a boned animal — chiefly poultry or fish filled with a forcemeat, rolled, tied, and poached in a suitable broth.

Giblets: Heart, liver, gizzard, and neck of poultry.

Glaze: A meat broth reduced until it becomes firm when cold, glaze is used to add flavor, color, and body to meats and sauces.

Mousse: A fine forcemeat that melts in the mouth, made from poultry, game, veal, liver or fish, and cream. A mousseline forcemeat can also be made from vegetables.

Pan-fry: To cook in hot fat in an open utensil.

Parfait: Forcemeat made from particularly fine ingredients, bound with gelatin or egg yolk, and sometimes lightened with whipped cream. A parfait can be turned out and cut into portions to serve.

Pâté: General term used in France to describe terrines, galantines, and *bouchée*. As a rule, however, it means a forcemeat, which is sometimes baked in dough.

Poach: To cook in liquid below boiling point.

Pot roasting: A means of stewing in which the food becomes lightly browned, used for light poultry meat, veal, fish, and game birds.

Quiche: Savory open-topped pie. The dough is prebaked blind to produce a crisp base.

Ragout: Braised dish made with pieces of meat, fish, or vegetables, bound with a seasoned sauce.

Reduce: To boil down to reduce the volume of liquid, to thicken it and intensify flavor.

Render: To melt solid fat.

Scallop: Very thin slice of meat, often beaten to make it even thinner.

Sear: To fry briefly in fat over a high heat, so that the surface is browned and seals in interior juices.

Skim: To remove excess fat. This can be done with a ladle or spoon, or with paper towels. Skimming can take place during cooking, but the simplest method is to let the liquid cool, then spoon off the surface layer of fat.

Steam: To cook in steam in a covered pot.

Stir-fry: To cook food quickly in a little hot fat in an open frying pan or wok, stirring constantly.

Stock: Liquid that is produced by boiling meat and/or bones and vegetables in water, which takes on the flavor of the food being cooked. Basic broth for soups and sauces.

Strain: To pour, rub or press a liquid, which can also contain cooked ingredients, through a strainer, sieve, or a cloth-lined sieve.

Sweat: To cook gently in a little fat and no liquid over a low heat, without the food browning.

Terrine: A forcemeat placed in a special mold lined with slices of bacon fat or foil and cooked in the oven in a *bain-marie*.

Timbale: A small cup-shaped mold or the dish made in such a mold.

Truss: To tie up poultry to achieve a desired shape for roasting.

Velouté: Basic white sauce.

Index of recipes